Schöningh
westermann

EinFach Englisch

Unterrichtsmodell

Series Editor: Hans Kröger

F. Scott Fitzgerald

The Great Gatsby

by
Daniela Franzen

edited by
Hans Kröger

Vorwort

Einzelarbeit

Partnerarbeit

Gruppen-
arbeit

Unterrichts-
gespräch

Schreib-
auftrag

Hausaufgabe

Audio-CD

filmische
Präsentation

Projekt, offene
Aufgabe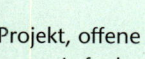

kreative
Aufgabe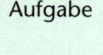

szenisches
Spiel,
Rollenspiel

Der Titel der Reihe **EinFach Englisch** verdeutlicht Zielsetzung und Programm zugleich. Einerseits soll Schülerinnen und Schülern auf einfache Art und Weise der Zugang zu klassischen, aber auch neuen literarischen Werken und Filmen ermöglicht werden, andererseits sollen Lehrerinnen und Lehrern in der Praxis erprobte Unterrichtsmodelle angeboten werden, die die wichtigsten methodisch-didaktischen Ansätze ihres Faches Englisch abdecken. Dabei sind die Modelle direkt, ohne langes Einlesen einsetzbar und stellen Unterrichtsarbeit konkret vor. Als besonders hilfreich für die Praxis haben sich dabei folgende Aspekte erwiesen, die für die Gestaltung der Reihe wesentlich sind:

- Überblick über **Figurenkonstellation**, ggf. **Filmszenen** und **Inhalt**
- **Klausuren** mit **Erwartungshorizont**
- **Arbeitsblätter**, **Tafelbilder** und **Leitfragen** für den Unterricht
- **Piktogramme** als Hinweise auf **Unterrichts-** und **Arbeitsformen**

Das Prinzip der „**Components**" ermöglicht darüber hinaus den variablen Einsatz der Modelle in unterschiedlich konzipierten Unterrichtsreihen. Dabei stehen Machbarkeit und Praxisnähe stets im Vordergrund.

> Das vorliegende Unterrichtsmodell bezieht sich auf folgende Textausgabe: F. Scott Fitzgerald: *The Great Gatsby*. Paderborn: Schöningh Verlag 2011. ISBN 978-3-14-041190-5

Sprachliche Betreuung: Anne Schülke

© 2019 Bildungshaus Schulbuchverlage Westermann Schroedel Diesterweg Schöningh Winklers GmbH, Georg-Westermann-Allee 66, 38104 Braunschweig
www.westermann.de

Druck A⁴ / Jahr 2023
Alle Drucke der Serie A sind im Unterricht parallel verwendbar.

Umschlaggestaltung: Jennifer Kirchhoff
Druck und Bindung: Westermann Druck Zwickau GmbH, Crimmitschauer Straße 43, 08058 Zwickau

ISBN 978-3-14-**041191**-2

Getting started

Then wear the gold hat, if that will
move her;
If you can bounce high, bounce for
her too,
Till she cry 'Lover, gold-hatted,
high bouncing lover,
I must have you!'

Thomas Parke D'Invilliers

I believe that on the first night I went
to Gatsby's house I was one of the few
guests who had actually been invited.
People were not invited – they went
there.

Nick

So we drove on toward death through
the cooling twilight.

Nick

They are a rotten crowd. You're worth
the whole damn bunch put together.

Nick to Gatsby

He thinks she goes to see her sister in
New York.
He's so dumb he doesn't know he's
alive.

Tom Buchanan

Can't repeat the past?... Why of course you can!
Gatsby

There must have been moments even that afternoon when Daisy tumbled short of his dreams – not through
her own fault but because of the colossal vitality of his illusion. It had gone beyond her, beyond everything.
He had thrown himself into it with a creative passion.
Fitzgerald, F. Scott: The Great Gatsby, pp. 69f.

Most of the big shore places were closed now and there were hardly any lights except the shadowy, moving
glow of a ferryboat across the Sound. And as the moon rose higher the inessential houses began to melt away
until gradually I became aware of the old island here that flowered once for Dutch sailors' eyes – a fresh, green
breast of the new world.
Fitzgerald, F. Scott: The Great Gatsby, p. 126

- What kind of novel do you think *The Great Gatsby* is?

- What issues are dealt with in *The Great Gatsby* as conveyed by the still, quotes
  and poem?

The Great Gatsby by F. Scott Fitzgerald

The novel 6
The author 6
The content 6
The characters 7

Das Unterrichtsmodell 10
Vorüberlegungen zum Einsatz des Romans im Unterricht 10
Konzeption des Unterrichtsmodells 11
Weiterführende Materialien 13

Klausuren 14

Component 1: Getting into the novel 22

1.1 Pre-reading activities 22
1.2 Long-term while-reading activities 23

Copy 1: Anticipation guide 27
Copy 2: Speculating & predicting 28
Copy 3: Literary terms to know: elements of fiction 30
Copy 4: Speculating & predicting: group work 31
Copy 5a: Presentations 32
Copy 5b: Understanding the time period – designing a stamp 33
Copy 6: While-reading task: chapter 1 34

Component 2: Who is who? Characters and conflicts 35

2.1 Completing a character map 35
2.2 Describing the characters (indirect and direct characterization) 36
2.3 Analysing the point of view 41
2.4 Describing and analysing the setting I (chapters 1 and 2) 44
2.5 Describing and analysing the setting II: Gatsby and his parties (chapter 3) 48

Copy 7: Character map 52
Copy 8: Describing characters 53
Copy 9: Nick Carraway – the ideal narrator? 54
Copy 10: While-reading task: chapter 2 55
Copy 11: Partying in New York City 56
Copy 12: Know the place! 57
Copy 13: While-reading task: chapter 3 58
Copy 14: Ain't we got fun?! 59

Component 3: A dream has come true? 60

3.1 Foreshadowing and predicting (chapter 4) 60
3.2 Playmaking: the reunion (chapter 5) 63
3.3 Analysing symbols 64
3.4 Understanding Gatsby's youth (chapter 6) 66

Copy 15: While-reading task: chapter 5 69
Copy 16: Playmaking: Read it out! Act it out! 70

Component 3: Continued

Copy 17: Symbolism **71**
Copy 18: While-reading task: chapter 6 **72**
Copy 19: The story of Gatsby's youth **73**

Component 4: Gatsby's fight for his dream **74**

4.1 Tom vs. Gatsby: structure of the plot (chapter 7) **74**
4.2 Writing a news story: the accident causing Myrtle's death **77**
4.3 Writing an analysis: symbolism **77**
4.4 Colours as symbols **78**
4.5 Evaluating Gatsby's character (chapter 8) **80**
4.6 Discussion: Who is to blame for Gatsby's death? **82**

Copy 20: The fight over Daisy **84**
Copy 21: Writing practice: analysing symbolism **85**
Copy 22: Colours as symbols **86**
Copy 23: Evaluating Gatsby **87**
Copy 24: Putting a character on trial **88**

Component 5: American dreams, American nightmares **89**

5.1 The ideal of the American Dream **89**
5.2 "They are careless people!" – dramatic reading **91**
5.3 Eulogy on the Great (?) Gatsby **92**
5.4 From dream to nightmare: the decline of the American Dream in the 1920s **93**

Copy 25: Benjamin Franklin: The way to wealth **95**
Copy 26: The ideal of the American Dream **96**
Copy 27: While-reading task: chapter 9 **97**
Copy 28: Dramatic reading **98**
Copy 29: How to write a eulogy **99**
Copy 30: Talking to the text **100**

Component 6: Post-reading activities **101**

6.1 Creative writing ideas **101**
6.2 The structure of the plot – a gallery walk **101**
6.3 Screen adaption **102**
6.4 The autobiographical background of the novel **103**

Copy 31: Screen adaption **104**

Component 7: Focus on language **105**

Copy 32: Connecting ideas (chapter 1) **109**
Copy 33: Stressing your message (chapter 3) **110**
Copy 34: Avoiding repetition (chapter 5) **111**
Copy 35: Using participle clauses (chapter 6) **112**
Copy 36: Focus on words: Brain 28 (chapters 2 and 3) **113**
Copy 37: Focus on words: adjectives (chapter 4) **114**
Copy 38: Focus on words: vocabulary replacement **115**

The novel

The author

F(rancis) Scott Key Fitzgerald (1896–1940) was an American writer of novels and short stories whose works are evocative of the Jazz Age, a term he coined himself. Although he led one of the wildest and most luxurious lifestyles of anyone during the 1920s, he was known more for his prominent works of literature, which have gained a permanent place among the American classics.

Born in St. Paul, Minnesota, to an upper-middle class Irish Catholic household, Fitzgerald was named after his famous relative, Francis Scott Key, the author of the National Anthem. Although the Fitzgeralds lived just blocks from the city's most elegant and wealthy families, they were not considered rich and therefore always tried hard to find their place in the community's social hierarchy. It seems likely much of Fitzgerald's interest in society life began in his youth when he would play and associate with the rich children of the neighbourhood – all the time knowing he was never entirely a part of their society.

In 1913, Fitzgerald entered Princeton University where he would not prove himself a top scholar but his literary achievements began to grow and he became friends with future critics and writers. In 1917 he was drafted into the army, but never participated in service abroad, instead spending much of his time writing his first novel, *This Side of Paradise*. First published in 1920, it became an instant success. In the same year, he married the beautiful Zelda Sayre and together they started a rich life of endless parties and extensive travelling to Europe. In many ways, the Fitzgeralds' extravagant lifestyle reads like something out of one of Scott's novels, and he himself was sometimes unsure "whether Zelda and I are real or whether we are characters in one of my novels." In order to escape the distractions of New York, Fitzgerald moved to France in 1924 to work on his novel, *The Great Gatsby*, which did not turn out to be as successful as his previous novels, but is today considered Fitzgerald's masterpiece.

Despite their celebrated status, the Fitzgeralds' domestic life was plagued with numerous difficulties. Throughout their marriage, both of them suffered from alcohol problems and Zelda was diagnosed with schizophrenia and eventually hospitalized. In addition, they faced financial difficulties since Fitzgerald's subsequent novels were not similarly successful. In order to maintain the extravagant lifestyle Zelda loved, Fitzgerald spent much time working on short stories that ran in popular magazines of the time such as *Cosmopolitan*. From 1930 until his death in 1940, Scott struggled to regain the stature he had earned with *The Great Gatsby*, but he never succeeded. He died of a heart attack and at that time, his books were out of print.

It was only during the late 1940s that a revival of Fitzgerald's works made both him and his novels more appreciated.

The content

F. Scott Fitzgerald's novel *The Great Gatsby* was written in 1925. While *The Great Gatsby* is a highly specific portrait of American society during the Roaring Twenties, its story is also one that has been told hundreds of times, and is perhaps as old as America itself: a man claws his way from rags to riches, only to find that his wealth cannot afford him the privileges enjoyed by those born into the upper class. The central character is Jay Gatsby, a wealthy New Yorker of indeterminate occupation. Gatsby is primarily known for the lavish parties he throws each weekend at his ostentatious Gothic mansion. He is suspected of being involved in illegal bootlegging and other underworld activities. One evening, the narrator, Nick Carraway, visits his cousin Daisy and her husband who live in the posh Long Island district of East Egg; Nick and Gatsby reside in nearby West Egg, a less fashionable area. At the Buchanan's, Nick is introduced to Jordan Baker with whom he begins a romantic relationship. Jordan tells him that Tom has a lover, Myrtle Wilson, who lives in the Valley of Ashes, a grey industrial area between West Egg and New York. Not long after this revelation, Nick travels to New York City with Tom and Myrtle. At a vulgar party in the apartment that Tom keeps for the affair, Myrtle begins to taunt Tom about Daisy, and Tom responds by breaking her nose. As the summer progresses, Nick eventually receives an invitation to one of Gatsby's legendary parties. Before the party, Nick himself had never met his neighbour in person but is now asked to come to his private rooms to speak with him alone. Later, Gatsby asks Nick to arrange a meeting between himself and Daisy, the love of his life. After an initially awkward reunion, Gatsby and Daisy restart their affair. After a short time, Tom grows increasingly suspicious of his wife's relationship to Gatsby. In front of Daisy, Nick and Jordan, he confronts Gatsby in a suite at a hotel and announces to his wife that Gatsby is a criminal. Daisy realizes that her real allegiance is to Tom and returns home, sharing a car with Gatsby. When the others drive through the Valley of Ashes, they discover that Gatsby's car has struck and killed Myrtle, Tom's lover. They rush back to Long Island, where Nick learns from Gatsby that Daisy was driving the car when it struck Myrtle, but that Gatsby intends to take the blame. The next day, Tom tells Myrtle's husband, George, that Gatsby was the driver of the car. George, desperate to find the killer, finds Gatsby in his pool and shoots him dead before committing suicide himself. After the murder, the Buchanans leave town, and Nick is left to organize Gatsby's funeral but finds that few people cared for him. He seeks out Gatsby's father, though, and brings him to New York. Thoroughly disgusted with the emptiness and moral decay of life among the wealthy on the East Coast, Nick decides to return to the Midwest. Before his departure, he sees the Buchanans once more who try to evoke Nick's sympathy.

The characters

Nick Carraway
Nick has a singular place within *The Great Gatsby*: he is both character and narrator of the story. A pretty solid young man (he turns thirty during the course of the novel) from Minnesota, Nick travels to New York in 1922 to learn the bond business. He rents the small house next to Gatsby's mansion in West Egg and, over the course of events, helps Gatsby reunite with Daisy, who happens to be Nick's cousin. As he tells the reader at the beginning of the novel, he is tolerant, open-minded, quiet and a good listener, and, as a result, others tend to talk to him and tell him their secrets. Gatsby, in particular, comes to trust him and treat him as a confidant. Insofar as Nick plays a role inside the narrative, he displays a strongly mixed reaction to life on the East Coast, one that creates a powerful internal conflict that he does not resolve until the end of the book. On the one hand, Nick is attracted to the fun-driven lifestyle of New York. On the other hand, he finds that lifestyle grotesque and damaging. This inner conflict is symbolized throughout the book by Nick's romantic affair with Jordan Baker. He is attracted to her vivacity and her sophistication just as he is repelled by her dishonesty and her lack of consideration for other people. After witnessing the unravelling of Gatsby's dream and his lonely death, he becomes disillusioned with how wealthy socialities like the Buchanans lead their lives. As a consequence, he returns to Minnesota in search of a quieter life.

Jay Gatsby (James Gatz)

Gatsby is both the novel's title character and its protagonist. He is a mysterious, newly wealthy young man. Every Saturday, his garish Gothic mansion in West Egg serves as the site of extravagant parties. Later, we learn that his real name is James Gatz; he was born in North Dakota to an impoverished farming family. While serving in the Army in World War I, Gatsby met Daisy Fay (now Daisy Buchanan) and fell passionately in love with her. Even though she had promised to wait for him until the end of the war, she got married to Tom Buchanan. After meeting Daisy, everything Gatsby did was for the single purpose of bringing her back into his life for good. Since money was, essentially, the cause of their separation, Gatsby made sure he would never again be without it. Gatsby's drive and perseverance in obtaining his goal is, in many ways, admirable. However, his money did not come from inheritance but from organized crime. By being so focused on his dream of Daisy, Gatsby moves further and further into a fantasy world. He is completely unable to realize that his dream is not reality and so stands watching for a sign from Daisy. What makes matters worse, too, is that he is in love with the idea of Daisy, not Daisy as she herself is.

Daisy Buchanan

Daisy is a beautiful young woman from Louisville, Kentucky. She is Nick's cousin and the object of Gatsby's love. As a young debutante in Louisville, Daisy was extremely popular among the military officers stationed near her home, including Jay Gatsby. Gatsby lied about his background to Daisy, claiming to be from a wealthy family in order to convince her that he was worthy of her. Eventually, Gatsby won Daisy's heart, and they made love before Gatsby left to fight in the war. Daisy promised to wait for Gatsby, but in 1919 she chose instead to marry Tom Buchanan, a young man from a solid, aristocratic family, who could promise her a wealthy lifestyle. After 1919, Gatsby dedicated himself to winning Daisy back, making her the single goal of all of his dreams and the main motivation behind his acquisition of immense wealth through criminal activity. In reality, however, Daisy falls far short of Gatsby's ideals. She is beautiful and charming, but also shallow, materialistic, bored and selfish. Daisy proves her real nature when she chooses Tom before Gatsby, then allows Gatsby to take the blame for killing Myrtle Wilson even though she herself was driving the car. She is fully aware of her husband's infidelities but ignores them because she enjoys the benefits of his money and power. Finally, rather than attending Gatsby's funeral, Daisy and Tom move away, leaving no forwarding address.

Tom Buchanan

Tom is Daisy's enormously wealthy husband, powerfully built and now leading a life of luxury in East Egg, playing polo, driving fast cars and riding horses. He is a former Yale football player who, like Daisy, comes from an immensely wealthy Midwestern family. He attracts attention through his boisterous and outspoken (even racist) behaviour and is proud of his many affairs. Even though he has no moral qualms about his affair with Myrtle Wilson, he becomes outraged and forces a confrontation when he suspects Daisy and Gatsby of having an affair. Tom as well as his wife are described as careless people who break things and then retreat into their wealth. It is Tom who, after Myrtle's death, tells Wilson that Gatsby was the killer and then hustles Daisy out of the area until the affair blows over.

Jordan Baker

Jordan Baker is Daisy's friend from Louisville and Nick's girlfriend during the summer of 1922. A competitive golfer, Jordan represents one of the "new women" of the 1920s – cynical, boyish, and self-centred. Jordan is beautiful but also dishonest: she cheated in order to win her first golf tournament and continually bends the truth.

Myrtle Wilson

Myrtle Wilson is Tom's lover, whose lifeless husband, George, owns a run-down garage in the Valley of Ashes. Myrtle herself possesses a fierce vitality and desperately looks for a way to improve her situation. Unfortunately for her, she chooses Tom, who treats her as a mere object of his desire. She eventually suffers a tragic end: after a fight with her husband, she runs out into the street and is hit and killed by Gatsby's car.

George Wilson

George Wilson is Myrtle's husband and the lifeless, exhausted owner of a run-down auto shop at the edge of the Valley of Ashes. George loves and idolizes Myrtle, and is devastated by her affair with Tom. When his wife is killed in a car accident, he is consumed with grief. On being told by Tom Buchanan that Gatsby caused his wife's death, he shoots him and then commits suicide.

Meyer Wolfshiem

A notorious underworld figure, Wolfshiem is a business associate of Gatsby. He is deeply involved in organized crime and even claims credit for fixing the 1919 World Series. His character, like Fitzgerald's view of the Roaring Twenties as a whole, is a curious mix of barbarism and refinement (his cuff links are made from human molars). After Gatsby's murder, however, Wolfshiem is one of the only people to express his grief or condolences; in contrast, the socially superior Buchanans fail to attend Gatsby's funeral.

Henry Gatz

Gatsby's father; his son's help is the only thing that saves him from poverty. Gatz tells Nick about his son's extravagant plans and dreams of self-improvement.

Das Unterrichtsmodell

Vorüberlegungen zum Einsatz des Romans im Unterricht

Die Geschichte von Jay Gatsby, einem einsamen reichen Geschäftsmann, der seiner längst verlorenen Liebe nachjagt, wurde zu einem der größten Klassiker der amerikanischen Literatur. Kaum ein amerikanischer Schüler kann von sich heute behaupten, dieser ‚Great American Novel' nicht während seiner Schullaufbahn begegnet zu sein.

Es sprechen viele Gründe dafür, diesen Roman auch im fremdsprachlichen Englischunterricht zu behandeln:

Unter landeskundlichen Aspekten bietet der Roman ein anschauliches und mitreißendes Gesellschaftsporträt der *Roaring Twenties*. Der Zeitgeist des *Jazz Age* mit seinen innovativen Musik- und Kunststilen, die Emanzipation der Frau, aber auch die Gegensätze zwischen Arm und Reich innerhalb der amerikanischen Gesellschaft sind nur eine kleine Auswahl an Aspekten, die der Film literarisch gestaltet.

Auf den ersten Blick ist der Roman thematisch natürlich zunächst eine tragische Liebesgeschichte: die des jungen Emporkömmlings Gatsby, der besessen von der Idee ist, seine große Liebe mit angehäuften Millionen für sich zu gewinnen. Damit bietet *The Great Gatsby* viele thematische Anknüpfungspunkte zum Themenbereich *Personal Relationships*, einem der Hauptthemen des Englischunterrichts der gymnasialen Oberstufe. Auch wenn die Hauptfiguren längst erwachsen sind, liegen zentrale Aspekte des Romans wie Glück und Scheitern, Träume, Identitätssuche und Sehnsucht wohl im Erfahrungsbereich der Schülerinnen und Schüler.

Auf den zweiten Blick handelt *The Great Gatsby* aber vor allem von dem zentralen Thema der amerikanischen Geschichte und Gegenwart, dem amerikanischen Traum, dessen Behandlung in keinem Rahmenplan des Englischunterrichts der Sekundarstufe II fehlt. Entlarvt wird der *American Dream* hier als das reine Verlangen nach Wohlstand, Reichtum und Vergnügen und ist damit weit entfernt von seinen ursprünglichen Idealen, wie dem Streben nach Freiheit und Glück. Die sozialkritische Dimension des Romans erschließt sich dem Leser allerdings nicht auf den ersten Blick, sodass die Thematisierung auch erst am Ende der Unterrichtseinheit unter Verwendung von Zusatzmaterial erfolgen kann.

Es handelt sich zwar um einen relativ kurzen, allerdings sprachlich sehr anspruchsvollen Roman. Dies liegt einerseits an der überaus metaphorischen und poetischen Sprache und den vielen symbolischen Anspielungen. Zum anderen ist die Handlungsstruktur äußerst komplex und von zahlreichen Rückblenden bestimmt. Es ist vor diesem Hintergrund daher sinnvoller, den Roman gemeinsam mit den Schülerinnen und Schülern sukzessive zu lesen und zu erarbeiten. Eine vorausgehende Lektüre würde die meisten Schülerinnen und Schüler sicher überfordern und damit demotivieren.

Ein zentrales Ziel des Unterrichtsmodells ist es, die Lektüre und das Verständnis dieses anspruchsvollen und facettenreichen Klassikers mittels vielfältiger Methoden und Aufgabentypen zu begleiten und zu erleichtern. Es wurde darauf geachtet, dass das Angebot an Aufgaben abwechslungsreich und an verschiedenen Lerntypen orientiert ist. Kooperative Lernformen, handlungs- und produktorientierte Verfahren wurden gezielt für das Unterrichtsmodell ausgesucht und auf den Roman zugeschnitten.

Es ist unvermeidlich, einzelne (sprachliche und inhaltliche) Aspekte des Romans unbeachtet zu lassen. Zu groß wäre sonst die Gefahr, dass die Schülerinnen und Schüler durch die Vielzahl an Themen verwirrt wären und den roten Faden verlieren. Die Reduzierung von inhaltlichen Aspekten liegt aber auch in der Notwendigkeit begründet, stärker auf die Schulung von bestimmten fremdsprachlichen Kompetenzen zu achten. Darin besteht ein weiterer zentrales Ziel des hier vorgestellten Unterrichtsmodells. Im Sinne eines kompetenzorientierten Englischunterrichts wurden bestimmte *skills* ausgewählt (*text analysis, how to write a summary, how to write a speech* etc.), die dann gezielt und exemplarisch am Roman geschult werden.

Abschließend sei aber darauf hingewiesen, dass die vorgestellten Vorschläge natürlich als Anregung zu verstehen sind, die hilfreich sein können, eine eigene, auf die jeweilige Schülergruppe abgestimmte Unterrichtsorganisation zu entwickeln.

Die Grundlage für das vorliegende Unterrichtsmodell bildet die annotierte Romanausgabe *The Great Gatsby,* die in der ‚EinFach Englisch'-Reihe des Schöningh Schulbuchverlages erschienen ist (2011).

Konzeption des Unterrichtsmodells

Das vorliegende Unterrichtsmodell ist so konzipiert, dass die einzelnen *Components* in chronologischer Reihenfolge, aber weitgehend variabel und abhängig von der individuellen Zielsetzung der Unterrichtsreihe eingesetzt werden können. Das Angebot an enthaltenen Arbeitsanregungen ist sehr umfangreich. In der zur Verfügung stehenden Unterrichtszeit wird es nicht möglich sein, alle hier vorgestellten Aufgaben in einem Kurs zu realisieren – damit würde sich die Lektüre und die Behandlung des Romans auch über alle Maßen in die Länge ziehen; dieses Unterrichtsmodell versteht sich in erster Linie als ein Angebot ganz unterschiedlicher Aufgaben und Unterrichtsarrangements, die eine ganze Bandbreite von Kompetenzen schulen sollen.

Component 1 bietet eine Auswahl an verschiedenen Zugängen zum Roman. Je nach Interesse der Lehrkräfte und der Schülerinnen und Schüler kann hier zwischen inhaltlichen, thematischen und literarischen Einstiegen gewählt werden. Dafür werden einige Zusatzmaterialien zur Verfügung gestellt, die z.T. auch in der Romanausgabe enthalten sind. Darüber hinaus werden einige *long-term reading tasks* präsentiert, die die ganze Unterrichtsreihe begleiten und ergänzen können.

Component 2 stellt die Hauptcharaktere und ihre Beziehungen zueinander in den Mittelpunkt der Betrachtung. Es werden Vorschläge für einen *long-term reading task* angeboten, die das Ziel verfolgen, eine Charakterisierung einer Hauptfigur zu verfassen. Des Weiteren erfolgt die Analyse zweier besonderer Merkmale des Romans: des *setting* sowie der Erzählperspektive. Dieser *Component* sollte komplett im Unterricht eingesetzt werden, um ein grundlegendes Verständnis der Handlung zu garantieren und um die Diskussion der sozialkritischen Dimension des Romans (siehe *Component 5)* vorzubereiten.

Component 3 bietet zum einen das Angebot einer szenischen Umsetzung einer Schlüsselszene des Romans, was möglicherweise eine willkommene Abwechslung im Leseprozess bedeutet. Zum anderen schulen die Schülerinnen und Schüler ihre Analysefähigkeiten, indem sie in einem *close-reading* wichtige Symbole erkennen und erläutern. Diese Kompetenz wird im nächsten *Component* weiter gefestigt.

Component 4 umfasst inhaltlich den dramatischen Höhepunkt des Romans, sodass sich eine Reihe von *while-reading tasks* sowie kreativer Schreibaufträge anbietet. Je nach Schwerpunktsetzung können unterschiedliche Aufgabenstellungen gekürzt werden.

Wie bereits erwähnt, steht auch in diesem *Component* die Textanalyse erneut im Vordergrund: Anhand einer Modellanalyse erarbeiten die Schülerinnen und Schüler wesentliche Elemente einer schriftlich verfassten Textanalyse und erhalten anschließend die Gelegenheit, ihre Kenntnisse gleich an einem neuen Beispiel anzuwenden.

In **Component 5** betrachten die Schülerinnen und Schüler den Roman als sozialkritischen Kommentar des Autors zum *American Dream* vor dem Hintergrund seiner Zeit. Dies erfolgt unter Einbeziehung einiger Zusatzmaterialien (Sachtext zum *American Dream*, Auszug aus der Biografie von Benjamin Franklin). Die in *Component 2* begonnene Vorbereitung der Figurenbeschreibung findet an dieser Stelle ihre Umsetzung auf das zentrale Thema des Romans. Die Arbeitsaufträge bereiten die Schülerinnen und Schüler thematisch auf die Klausuren vor.

Component 6 ist optional einsetzbar und bietet eine Reihe von verschiedenen Vorschlägen zur Nachbereitung des Romans (kreatives Schreiben, Verfassen eines Drehbuchauszugs, eine Analyse der Handlungsstruktur, eine Textarbeit zur autobiografischen Komponente des Romans).

Component 7 bietet verschiedene Übungen, die die sprachliche Ausdrucksfähigkeit der Schülerinnen und Schüler verbessern sollen und die während der Lektürearbeit eingesetzt werden können. Alle Vorschläge beziehen sich gezielt auf bestimmte Kapitel des Romans und ergänzen den Literaturunterricht.

Weiterführende Materialien

Interpretationshilfen

Abbot, A.: *Lektürehilfen F. Scott Fitzgerald „The Great Gatsby"*. Stuttgart: Ernst Klett Verlag 1994.

Hoops, T. & Hoops, W.: *The Great Gatsby. Teacher's Guide*. Stuttgart: Ernst Klett Verlag 1995.

Fachdidaktische Materialien & Unterrichtsvorschläge

Bamford, Julian & Richard R. Day: *Extensive Reading Activities for Teaching Language*. Cambridge University Press 2004.

Bowers, Kristen: *The Great Gatsby by F. Scott Fitzgerald: Literature Guide*. Secondary Solutions 2009.

Collett, Jessica: *Read With Me. A Guide to Strategic Reading*. Learn With Me, LLC 2010.

Collie, J./Slater, S.: *Literature in the Language Classroom. A resource book of ideas and activities*. Cambridge University Press 2001.

Duff, Alan & Alan Maley: *Literature*. Oxford University Press 2007.

Greenwood, Jean: *Class Readers*. Oxford University Press 2001.

Griesel-Kindel, C./Henseler, R./Möller, S.: *Method Guide. Schüleraktivierende Methoden für den Englischunterricht in den Klassen 5 – 10*. Paderborn: Schöningh 2007.

Griesel-Kindel, C./Henseler, R./Möller, S.: *Method Guide. Methoden für einen kooperativen und individualisierenden Englischunterricht in den Klassen 5 – 12*. Paderborn: Schöningh 2009.

Handke, Ulrike: *Mehr Erfolg im Unterricht*. Cornelsen Scriptor 2008.

Schallhorn, K./Peschel, A.: *Method Guide. Kreative Methoden für den Englischunterricht in der Oberstufe*. Paderborn: Schöningh 2004.

Sicher ins Zentralabitur. Stuttgart: Ernst Klett Verlag 2006.

Spann, E.: *Abiturwissen Landeskunde Great Britain & United States of America*. Stuttgart: Ernst Klett Verlag 2000.

Klausuren

Im Folgenden finden sich zwei Klausurvorschläge, die nach der Bearbeitung des Unterrichtsmodells einsetzbar sind. **Klausur 1** (Leistungskursbereich) bezieht sich auf einen Auszug aus dem letzten Kapitel des Romans und stellt die Sozialkritik des Autors in den Mittelpunkt der Betrachtung. Die Aufgabenstellung berücksichtigt unter 2. die Konzeption des Unterrichtsmodells, indem die Schülerinnen und Schüler die Möglichkeit haben, sich auf zwei Charaktere zu beschränken. Die Erörterung des Romantitels zielt auf die kritische Auseinandersetzung mit der Hauptfigur ab. Es wäre denkbar, die Aufgabenstellung noch um eine kreative Komponente zu erweitern, indem die Schülerinnen und Schüler einen eigenen Titelvorschlag präsentieren und auf der Basis der Lektüre begründen.

Textgrundlage der **Klausur 2** (Grundkursbereich) ist ein amerikanischer Zeitungsartikel aus dem Jahr 2008, in dem es um die menschlichen Folgen der weltweiten Immobilien- und Finanzkrise geht. Im Zentrum dieses Vorschlags steht damit die aktuelle Relevanz und der Bezug zur Gegenwart dieses Klassikers. Voraussetzung für diese Klausur ist, dass im Unterricht die Analyse und eigene Produktion von Zeitungsartikeln durchgenommen wurde (siehe *Component 4.2*). Auch ist es vorteilhaft, wenn die Schülerinnen und Schüler über grobe Kenntnisse über die Hintergründe der Finanzkrise verfügten. Die kreative Schreibaufgabe erfolgt für leistungsschwächere Kurse in enger Anlehnung an das Unterrichtsmodell.

The moral geography

The following extract is taken from the last chapter of the novel *The Great Gatsby*. In the closing pages, Nick, the narrator, turns inward and talks about the situation after Gatsby's death:

I see now that this has been a story of the West, after all – Tom and Gatsby, Daisy and Jordan and I, were all Westerners, and perhaps we possessed some deficiency in common which made us subtly unadaptable to Eastern life.

5 Even when the East excited me most, even when I was most keenly aware of its superiority to the bored, sprawling, swollen towns behind the Ohio, with their interminable inquisitions which spared only the children and the very old – even then it had always for me a quality of distortion. West Egg, especially, still figures in my more fantastic dreams. I see it as a night scene by El Greco: a hundred houses, at once conventional and grotesque, crouching under a sullen, overhanging sky and a lustreless

10 moon. In the foreground four solemn men in dress suits are walking along the sidewalk with a stretcher on which lies a drunken woman in a white evening dress. Her hand, which dangles over the side, sparkles cold with jewels. Gravely the men turn in at a house – the wrong house. But no one knows the woman's name, and no one cares.

15 After Gatsby's death the East was haunted for me like that, distorted beyond my eyes' power of correction. So when the blue smoke of brittle leaves was in the air and the wind blew the wet laundry stiff on the line I decided to come back home.

[...]

One afternoon late in October I saw Tom Buchanan. He was walking ahead of me along

20 Fifth Avenue in his alert, aggressive way, his hands out a little from his body as if to fight off interference, his head moving sharply here and there, adapting itself to his restless eyes. Just as I slowed up to avoid overtaking him he stopped and began frowning into the windows of a jewellery store. Suddenly he saw me and walked back holding his hand.

25 'What's the matter, Nick? Do you object to shaking hands with me?'

'Yes. You know what I think of you.'

'You're crazy, Nick,' he said quickly. 'Crazy as hell. I don't know what's the matter with you.'

'Tom,' I inquired, 'what did you say to Wilson that afternoon?'

30 He stared at me without a word, and I knew I had guessed right about those missing hours. I started to turn away, but he took a step after me and grabbed my arm.

'I told him the truth,' he said. 'He came to the door while we were getting ready to leave, and when I sent down the word that we weren't in he tried to force his way upstairs. He was crazy enough to kill me if I hadn't told him who owned the car. His hand

35 was on a revolver in his pocket every minute he was in the house –' He broke off defiantly. 'What if I did tell him? That fellow had it coming to him. He threw dust into your eyes just like he did in Daisy's, but he was a tough one. He ran over Myrtle like you'd run over a dog and never even stopped his car.'

There was nothing I could say, except the one unutterable fact that it wasn't true.

40 'And if you think I didn't have my share of suffering – look here, when I went to give up that flat and saw that damn box of dog biscuits sitting there on the sideboard, I sat down and cried like a baby. By God it was awful –'

I couldn't forgive him or like him, but I saw that what he had done was, to him, entirely justified. It was all very careless and confused. They were careless people, Tom

45 and Daisy – they smashed up things and creatures and then retreated back into their money or their vast carelessness, or whatever it was that kept them together, and let other people clean up the mess they had made …

sprawling spread out in a disorganized way over a large area
interminable endless
inquisition investigation to discover any unusual or immoral behaviour or beliefs
distortion being twisted out of shape
El Greco (1541–1616) Greek painter, used distorted figures and a contrast between bright colours and grey to express religious ecstasy
lustreless not bright
brittle likely to break because of being dry and cold
alert watchful

defiant showing strong resistance

share part, portion

I shook hands with him; it seemed silly not to, for I felt suddenly as though I were talking to a child. Then he went into the jewellery store to buy a pearl necklace – or perhaps only a pair of cuff buttons – rid of my provincial squeamishness for ever.

cuff button *Manschetten-knopf*

Fitzgerald, F. Scott: The Great Gatsby, Paderborn: Schöningh Verlag 2001, pp. 124–126

Assignments

1. Summarize the content of the given extract of the novel *The Great Gatsby* by F. Scott Fitzgerald in your own words. (Comprehension)

2. "I see now that this has been a story of the West, after all – Tom and Gatsby, Daisy and Jordan and I, were all Westerners, and perhaps we possessed some deficiency in common which made us subtly unadaptable to Eastern life."

   Fitzgerald, F. Scott: The Great Gatsby, Paderborn: Schöningh Verlag 2011, p. 124

   Explain Nick's statement by describing two of the characters in detail as they are presented in the novel. (Analysis)

3. F. Scott Fitzgerald was always ambivalent about the title of his novel, shifting from *Gatsby*, to *Among Ash-Heaps and Millionaires*, to *The High-Bouncing Lover*, to *Under the Red, White and Blue*.
   Comment on Fitzgerald's final decision: Do you think it is a suitable title for the novel? (Comment)

Erwartungshorizont zu Klausur 1

Zu 1:
- Nick decides to leave the East and to return home to the Midwest.
- The East attracts him because of its excitement which contrasts with the boredom and provincial character of the Midwest.
- After Gatsby's death, though, the East repels him because of its apparent lack of morals and concern for other people, and the excess of pleasure, senseless drinking, and decadent parties.
- Nick runs into Tom one day and questions him about his confrontation with Wilson before Gatsby's death.
- Tom defends himself; he believes that his actions were justified.
- Even though Nick blames Tom for Gatsby's death (it was Tom who told Wilson that Gatsby owned the car), he cannot really argue with Tom or get mad at him.
- Tom and Nick don't share the same moral standards.

Zu 2: Explanation of the quotation:
- It expresses Nick's criticism of the people who moved East in pursuit of a new dream of money, fame, success, glamour, and excitement.
- Life in the East is characterized by a corruption of the American Dream (= pursuit of happiness, strong belief in success and freedom): pursuit of power and pleasure, an empty form of success.

Character analysis:
Für eine detaillierte Analyse der Charaktere sei auf die Charakterbeschreibungen ("plot and characters") verwiesen. Die Darstellung und die ausgewählten Beispiele sollten sich auf das Zitat beziehen und die Kritik an der Gesellschaft im Allgemeinen zum Ausdruck bringen.

Zu 3: Folgende Aspekte sind erwähnenswert:
- The title character is neither "great" nor named Gatsby; he is a criminal whose real name is James Gatz, and the life he has created for himself is an illusion.
- Nick is particularly taken with Gatsby and considers him a great figure: he sees both the extraordinary quality of hope that Gatsby possesses and his idealistic dream of loving Daisy in a perfect world.
- Though Nick recognizes Gatsby's flaws the first time he meets him, he cannot help but admire Gatsby's brilliant smile, his romantic idolization of Daisy, and his yearning for the future.
- Nick alone among the novel's characters recognizes that Gatsby's love for Daisy has less to do with Daisy's inner qualities than with Gatsby's own. That is, Gatsby makes Daisy his dream because his heart demands a dream, not because Daisy truly deserves the passion that Gatsby feels for her.
- Furthermore, Gatsby impresses Nick with his power to make his dreams come true: He dreams of Daisy, and for a while he wins her, too.
- In a world without a moral centre, in which attempting to fulfil one's dreams is like rowing a boat against the current, Gatsby's power to dream lifts him above the meaningless and amoral pleasure seeking of the New York society. In Nick's view, Gatsby's capacity to dream makes him "great" despite his flaws and eventual undoing.

Murder-Suicide in California:
A Tragedy of the Financial Crisis?

By Alison Stateman/Sorrento Pointe for TIME Magazine, Oct. 8, 2008

Sorrento Pointe, Calif., does not look like the setting for the death of the American Dream. From outside the tasteful guardhouse stationed at the entrance of this gated community about 23 miles from downtown Los Angeles, all seems peaceful. The man-icured lawns are a verdant oasis within the surrounding sun-scorched mountains. The **verdant** here: green

5 only sound disturbing the quiet is the gentle swish of luxury cars – Mercedes, BMWs and Porsches – as their drivers turn homeward.

However, that sense of well-being was shattered brutally on Monday, Oct. 6, when po-lice discovered the bodies of the Rajaram family in their home on Como Lane. Karthik Rajaram, 45, had shot his mother-in-law, wife and three children to death before kill-

10 ing himself sometime between Saturday evening and Monday morning.

Rajaram, a former financial analyst at PricewaterhouseCoopers and Sony Pictures, left two suicide notes – one for police and another for family and friends – and a will. „I understand he was unemployed, his dealings in the stock market had taken a disastrous turn for the worse," said Los Angeles deputy police chief Michel R. Moore. „This was a

15 person who had been quite successful in this arena." Amid news of the global financial **amid** among

crisis and the credit crunch, this murder-suicide has become emblematic of the times – **credit crunch** credit crisis

in its way paralleling the deathly plunges of Wall Street stockbrokers in 1929. **emblematic** symbolic of
plunge fall

Rajaram's had been something of an immigrant-American success story. Born in India, he grew up in Bangalore and graduated in 1985 from the now famous Indian Institute

20 of Technology in Chennai (formerly Madras). He went to Los Angeles to earn an M.B.A. **M.B.A.** Master of
from UCLA before working at Sony Pictures from 1989 to 1994, according to a com- Business Administration
pany spokesman. He went on to serve in a small consulting group within Pricewater- (university degree)
houseCoopers dedicated to strategy and operational consulting for motion-picture **UCLA** University of
companies. He left in 1999 to join EHS Partners, a start-up consulting firm. A 2001 California (Los Angeles)

25 story in the *Daily Telegraph* of London, under the headline "Bust, but big bucks for the **PricewaterhouseCoop-**
big boys," called Rajaram a "winner" in a deal for NanoUniverse, a Los Angeles- and **ers** influential and
London-based venture fund taken public on the London Stock Exchange, the Los An- well-known consulting
geles *Times* reported. For a 12,500-pound investment, Rajaram, one of the company's company
founders, received 875,000 pounds – or about $1.2 million in 2001 dollars – after a

30 voluntary liquidation, the *Telegraph* reported. **liquidation** closing of a
business
Rajaram had even been lucky just before California's housing bubble burst, according **housing bubble**
to his former Northridge neighbor and real estate agent Sue Karns. He sold his home *Immobilienblase*
two years ago for $750,000, making a sizable profit on the property he and his wife had purchased in 1997 for $274,000, according to The Los Angeles *Times*. He then moved

35 to the Sorrento Pointe house, planning to rent for a few years before buying again.

Despite his record of success at holding executive-level jobs and making highly profit-able investments, Rajaram had apparently been unable to find work. Meanwhile, he began to accumulate financial losses which took their toll on his saved-up profits. Sud- **to take its toll** seinen/
denly having an M.B.A., working one's way up in finance and using one's business *ihren Tribut fordern*

40 acumen to make solid investments offered little protection and security. "The essence **acumen** cleverness
of it was that this was a man's emotional spiral downward due to financial difficulties. He saw it as a tragedy, a disaster that had befallen him. He lost perspective," said the LAPD's Moore. "He thought his life circumstances were because he was a failure. He got caught up in a rabbit hole, apart from reality."

45 [...] Another former PricewaterhouseCoopers colleague and friend, David Gerken, who last spoke to Rajaram 18 months ago, says Rajaram took his career and family very seri-ously and wanted to do right by them. Perhaps it was this self-induced pressure that proved to be too much, warping his perspective and making his final violent act seem **to warp** *sich krümmen*
justifiable. "The last time I spoke with him, he had been out of work for a while. He was

50 concerned about how the situation was impacting his family but seemed to be taking things in stride," says Gerken. "There was no indication of how serious it was or any suggestion of what would happen. It speaks to the desperation he must have felt."

Assignments

1. Sum up the article in your own words. *(Comprehension)*

2. Analyse the structure and the language of the article. What rhetorical devices does the author employ to create her intended effect? *(Analysis)*

3. Choose one of the following tasks:

   a) Remember the evidence surrounding the death of Gatsby or George Wilson. Write a newspaper article about one of the two tragic deaths as it might appear in a quality or popular paper. Use the journalistic style your newspaper demands (intention, addressee, register, style, content, headline etc.) *(Re-creation of text)*

   b) Today, the novel *The Great Gatsby* is widely regarded as a "great American novel" and a timeless literary classic. Comment on this statement by referring to the article as well as the novel. *(Comment)*

Erwartungshorizont zu Klausur 2

Zu 1:
- The article is about the tragic murder-suicide of a family from California in October 2008.
- Rajaram, born in India and a formerly successful financial analyst employed by numerous well-known US American companies, kills his wife, his mother-in-law and his three children before committing suicide himself.
- He is a well-educated analyst and clever businessman in the field of investment and housing.
- However, due to the worldwide economic crisis he becomes and remains unemployed until the fatal incidents of October 2008.
- As time goes by, he loses more and more of his savings and is finally unable to support his family.
- Apparently, he loses perspective and becomes increasingly pessimistic and hopeless concerning his future. He seems to be unable to confront his own family with the reality of their situation.
- He is described as a sensitive, caring family man who cannot deal with the pressure resulting from his financial situation.

Zu 2:
- overall effect of the article: presenting the fatal and tragic human consequences of the worldwide economic crisis
- type of text: news story (longer than a report because it includes background information); quality paper: clear separation of facts and opinion
- structure: first three paragraphs answer all the 'wh'-questions as well as the intention of the author (see above); additional information (background information and comments) is given towards the end of the article (example: family background, Rajaram's educational and professional career, comment by friend and colleague).
- language: formal and precise language, complex syntax and rhetorical devices, consistent with the level of their readership, quotations and use of direct speech.
- strict separation between facts and opinion

Folgende Textbelege sind erwähnenswert:
- **complex sentence structures:** subordinate clauses (l. 45: "David Gerken, who ..."), participle constructions (l. 32f.: "He sold his home ..., making a sizable profit ..."), infinitive constructions (l. 20: "He went to LA to earn an ...")
- **quotations/direct speech (instead of reported speech):** l. 40ff. and 49ff.: to appear authentic and credible.
- **register/choice of words:** "to purchase", "executive-level jobs", "to accumulate financial losses" etc.
- **rhetorical devices:** rhetorical question (headline) to appeal to the reader; contrasting phrases and expressions in the first paragraph to emphasize the tragedy (tasteful, peaceful, verdant oasis etc. versus death, shattered brutally, had shot to death etc.); alliterations: "the surrounding sun-scorched mountains", "financial crisis and credit crunch"; enumerations: "Mercedes, BMWs and Porsches"; comparisons/allusions: "paralleling the deathly plunges of Wall Street stockbrokers in 1929."

Zu 3: a) Folgende Aspekte sollten Berücksichtigung finden:
Inhalt:

- kurzer Bericht über die Tat (who, what, when, where, why),
- Hintergrundinformationen über den Tathergang, Ausblick (mögliche Täter, Festnahmen, Zeugenaussagen, Polizeiberichte etc.).

Sprache:

- der Zeitungsart angemessene Sprache: Wortschatz, Satzbau, rhetorische Mittel,
- passende Überschrift.

b) Folgende Aspekte sollten Berücksichtigung finden:
parallels between two texts:

- **dream:** Rajaram wanted to live the American Dream (he was an immigrant to the US), dream of financial success, wealth, ...
- **weakness/inability:** Rajaram was unable to confront the problems, the reality of his situation, chose to die instead of accepting his failure
- **responsibility:** Rajaram was (probably) not responsible for his failure (world wide economic crisis)

Getting into the novel

1.1 Pre-reading activities

Anticipation guide (focus on themes)

Ein möglicher thematischer Einstieg in die Unterrichtsarbeit ist der sogenannte *anticipation guide*, der auf der *think-pair-share*-Methode beruht. Die Schülerinnen und Schüler beziehen zunächst individuell Stellung zu den aufgeführten Aussagen, die alle mit den wichtigsten *themes* des Romans in Verbindung stehen *(Copy 1)*. Im Anschluss daran tauschen sie sich über ihre Einstellung in Gruppen aus, dokumentieren ihre Ergebnisse und erörtern Unterschiede und Gemeinsamkeiten. Abschließend reflektieren die Schüler gemeinsam ihren Diskussionsprozess und fassen ihre Ergebnisse schriftlich zusammen. Wichtig ist, dass die Arbeitsmaterialien am Ende der Stunde vom Lehrer wieder eingesammelt werden, um sie dann nach der Unterrichtseinheit erneut zu besprechen. So lässt sich feststellen, ob sich durch die Lektüre Meinungen und Einstellungen verändert haben und weshalb.

Diese *activity* eignet sich nicht nur hervorragend für einen thematischen Einstieg in den Roman, sondern garantiert auch einen regen Austausch unter den Schülerinnen und Schülern und bildet einen klaren roten Faden für die ganze folgende Unterrichtsarbeit.

Now discuss those issues on which your group was divided. Present your own arguments and listen carefully to your classmates' responses.

After discussing all controversial issues, answer the questions given below on the backside of the page. Be sure to use complete sentences.

1. Which statement triggered off the most interesting or controversial discussion?

2. Was any argument strong enough to make you change your mind or want to change any of your initial responses? Why or why not?

3. What were some of the strongest or most memorable points made by you or your group members?

4. Which statement triggered off an emotional discussion? Why do you think it happened?

Your teacher will collect and keep your charts and responses to use after you have finished reading the novel.

Post-reading: individual reflection

Now that you have completed the novel *The Great Gatsby*, complete the right-hand column ("After Reading" column) of the Anticipation Guide and reread your responses after the group discussion.

Then answer the following questions on a separate sheet of paper.

1. How many of your answers have changed since reading the novel?

2. Which statements do you see differently now and what made you think differently?

3. Describe an important event, conversation etc. of the novel that affected you and your previous opinion.

4. Which of your answers were supported by the content of the novel? Give one example.

Compare and discuss your results in a small group:

1. How are your responses different after reading the novel?

2. How do you explain these different opinions and viewpoints?

Predicting & speculating activity (focus on plot & setting)

Die im Folgenden beschriebene *predicting & speculating activity* ermöglicht einen inhaltlichen Einstieg in die Lektüre. Die Schülerinnen und Schüler erhalten jeweils ein Informationsmaterial zum Roman, das sie individuell bearbeiten und für die nächste Phase vorbereiten:

1. The Jazz Age (siehe S. 129/130 der Romanausgabe)
2. The author (siehe S. 128/129 der Romanausgabe)
3. some quotes (s. "Getting Started"-Seiten)
4. some stills from the movie

Die Arbeitsaufträge zu den Informationstexten 1–3, die in der Romanausgabe vorliegen, befinden sich auf **Copy 2**.

In der nun folgenden Gruppenarbeit stellen die Schülerinnen und Schüler sich gegenseitig ihre Ergebnisse vor und erarbeiten dann gemeinsam – auf der Grundlage ihrer individuellen Arbeitsergebnisse – eine mögliche Romanzusammenfassung *(Copy 4)*. In diesem Zusammenhang bietet es sich an, relevante fiktionale Elemente zu reaktivieren und von den Schülerinnen und Schülern kreativ bestimmen zu lassen (siehe Einleitung **Copy 3**). Falls die Schülerinnen und Schüler zuvor den oben vorgestellten *anticipating guide* diskutiert haben, können sie natürlich auch aufgefordert werden, die aufgeworfenen *themes* mit einfließen zu lassen.

Relevante Redemittel für die Erarbeitungsphase in den Gruppen sollten den Schülerinnen und Schülern an die Hand gegeben werden, um eine einsprachige und konstruktive Diskussion zu ermöglichen.

Additional presentations

Die *speculating & predicting activity* kann selbstverständlich durch weitere Schülervorträge erweitert werden, in denen einzelne Aspekte des *Jazz Age* vertieft werden. Gewinnbringend sind folgende Aspekte:

- Prohibition, speakeasies and the bootlegger
- Music and dancing in the *Roaring Twenties*
- Fashion trends of the 1920s
- Women's rights, suffrage and important women of the 1920s
- Gangsters: Al Capone, John Dillinger, Lucky Luciano
- The Red Scare and Communism
- Sports and sports stars of the 1920s

- Ford, the assembly line and the first automobiles
- Flapper culture and lifestyle
- Theatre, film, and radio of the 1920s
- Black Friday and the Great Depression
  …

1.2 Long-term while-reading activities

Die Lektüre des Romans ist für viele Schülerinnen und Schüler sprachlich und inhaltlich sicherlich eine große Herausforderung. Um sie während des Lesens zu unterstützen und ihnen ein aktives und positives Lernerlebnis zu verschaffen, werden im Folgenden eine Reihe von langfristigen *while-reading activities* präsentiert, die je nach Leistungsstand der Schülerinnen und Schüler miteinander kombiniert oder auch einzeln eingesetzt werden können. Zur Vorbereitung auf die jeweiligen Einzelstunden, in denen einzelne Kapitel behandelt werden, werden darüber hinaus pro Kapitel *reading comprehension tasks* vorgestellt.

Vor dem Hintergrund dieser Möglichkeiten ist es daher notwendig, vor Beginn der Unterrichtseinheit eine für die Schülergruppe angemessene und abwechslungsreiche Auswahl an langfristigen und kurzfristigen Leseaufträgen auszusuchen.

Reading log

Als begleitende Aufgabe führen die Schülerinnen und Schüler ein *reading log*, das durchaus auch über die bloße Textzusammenfassung der neun Kapitel hinausgehen kann.
Folgende Fragestellungen sichern eine aktive, individualisierte Lektüre:

SUMMARIZE	In your own words, retell the action and important details of your reading (one paragraph of 5 – 7 sentences).
QUESTION	Write down questions you have about this chapter, and about the reading that you do not understand and/or would like your teacher to clarify.
CONNECT	Try to relate the characters or events to some aspect of your own life or world around you. Has this or something like this ever happened to you? How did you handle this situation = Have you ever known a person like any of the characters?
PREDICT	Try to make a guess or prediction as to what may happen in the next chapter. What effect will this event have on those involved?
REFLECT	After reading this chapter, finish these sentences I learned … I was surprised … I wonder … I feel … I enjoyed …
RECORD	Choose one quote from this chapter you feel is important or significant. In addition to writing the quote, record the character who said it, the context in which it was spoken, and the page number.

Die Schüler legen eine Tabelle mit den ausgewählten Fragestellungen an und vervollständigen diese für jedes gelesene Kapitel des Romans.

Reading journal

Eine weitere Aufgabe, die die Schülerinnen und Schüler während der Lektüre motiviert und vor allem aber das Lesen individualisiert, ist das Verfassen eines *reading journals* (Lesetagebuch).

In einem separaten Hefter oder Heft notieren die Schülerinnen und Schüler ihre persönlichen Leseerfahrungen und spontanen Eindrücke und ihre Einstellungen zu Thesen und Kontroversen, die der Roman aufwirft. Dies kann ganz konventionell nach jedem Kapitel erfolgen; eine interessante Alternative ist es aber auch, die Tagebücher als Lehrkraft aufzubewahren und an die Schülerinnen und Schüler für kurze Schreibphasen zu verteilen, in denen sie dann kurz (für ca. 10 Min.) ihre persönlichen Gedanken zu einer speziellen Frage, die im Zusammenhang mit dem gerade im Zentrum stehenden Inhalt notieren. Diese Aufgabe kann als *pre-, while-* und auch *post-reading task* eingesetzt werden. Wichtig ist, dass den Schülerinnen und Schülern vorher gesagt wird, dass die Ergebnisse nicht kontrolliert oder korrigiert werden; sie werden lediglich eingesammelt und können am Ende der Unterrichtsreihe, des Schulhalbjahres oder sogar der Schulzeit als Erinnerung zurückgegeben werden. Es ist auch denkbar, alle weiteren Schülerprodukte, Fotos der Unterrichtsarbeit o. Ä. zu integrieren. Gerade weil die *writing prompts* übergeordnete und generelle Fragestellungen tangieren, erhalten die Schülerinnen und Schüler ein interessantes Porträt ihrer Gedankenwelt.

Im weiteren Verlauf des Unterrichtsmodells werden im Folgenden für die einzelnen Kapitel *writing prompts*, die speziell für das *reading journal* geeignet sind, unter der Rubrik *Read and Respond* vorgestellt.

Vocabulary

Der Roman ist sprachlich sehr anspruchsvoll, sodass die annotierte Version zu bevorzugen ist. Die diesem Unterrichtsmodell zugrunde liegende Romanausgabe weist spezielles Lernvokabular aus, das die Schülerinnen und Schüler langfristig behalten und verwenden sollen. Im Folgenden finden sich eine Reihe bewährter *activities*, die die Wortschatzarbeit auch in der Oberstufe abwechslungsreicher gestalten können. Es ist denkbar, für jedes Kapitel einen anderen Aufgabentyp auszuwählen oder den Schülern selbst die Entscheidung zu überlassen, welche *activity* sie je nach Lerntyp bevorzugen.

- Draw a picture depicting the word.
- Finish the following statement: *This word reminds me of …*
- Write the definition in your own words.
- Find two synonyms and two antonyms for each word.
- Pretend you are a newscaster and write headlines using the words.
- Look up the etymology of the word.
- Use the word in a sentence (Be sure that the sentence deals with the topic of the novel).
- …

20-second-presentations

Eines der besonderen Merkmale des Romans ist seine Fülle an Details und Anspielungen, die dem Leser die *Roaring Twenties* näher bringen. Es ist daher lohnend, die sprachlichen Feinheiten visuell im Unterricht zu präsentieren. Die annotierte Romanausgabe bietet zwar in fast allen Fällen genaue Beschreibungen der für diese Zeit spezifischen Phänomene, allerdings lässt sich der Zeitgeist noch stärker durch Bild- oder Tonmaterial vermitteln. Dies kann in der Einstiegsphase durch Kurzpräsentationen erfolgen.

Copy 5a enthält eine Liste von Hintergrundereignissen, Alltagsgegenständen und spezifischen Phänomenen der Zwanzigerjahre. Die Schülerinnen und Schüler wählen ein Thema/Objekt aus und präsentieren dieses mithilfe eines Bildes in wenigen Sekunden. Alternativ können die Kurzpräsentationen auch analog zur Lektüre erfolgen (z. B. in der Einstiegsphase einer bestimmten Stunde).

Alternativ kann nach der *pre-reading*-Phase auch eine kreative Umsetzung der Ära des *Jazz Age* unter Einbeziehung aller thematischen Aspekte erfolgen: Die Schülerinnen und Schüler erhalten den Auftrag, eine Briefmarke für die Epoche zu kreieren (siehe *Copy 5b*). Die Präsentation der Ergebnisse kann in Form einer Rede erfolgen, in der sie ihre Motivwahl verteidigen müssen.

Am Ende der Einstiegsphase erhalten die Schülerinnen und Schüler die Aufgabe, das erste Kapitel des Romans zu Hause zu lesen. Zur Sicherung des Leseverständnisses vervollständigen sie *Copy 6*.

Anticipation guide

Before you start reading the novel *The Great Gatsby* think about the ten statements and proverbs given below and decide individually if you agree or disagree with the statements. You may also decide to remain unsure about some of them. Complete the left-hand column ("Before Reading" column) by using the corresponding symbols:

+ = I agree   **– = I disagree**   **? = I don't know**

Before Reading	Statement	After Reading
	1. Money is the root of all evil.	
	2. You cannot relive the past.	
	3. Love conquers all.	
	4. Love cannot exist without trust.	
	5. Poverty equals unhappiness.	
	6. People usually get what they deserve.	
	7. Most people want to be rich, powerful and respected.	
	8. The American Dream has run out of gas. The car has stopped.	
	9. To believe in one's dreams is to spend all of one's life asleep.	
	10. Hard work alone determines success.	

After completing the left-hand column, get into small groups and collect the number of students who oppose, support or feel unsure about each statement. Sum up your group result in the table given below.

Group members: _____

Statement	+	–	?
1			
2			
3			
4			
5			
6			
7			
8			
9			
10			

Speculating & predicting

Your task is to speculate on what the novel *The Great Gatsby* is about. Each member of your group focuses on a different set of information:

a) the Jazz Age, b) <u>the author</u>, c) some quotes, d) some stills from the movie.

Read your set of information on page 128/129 of your novel and complete the comprehension tasks given below. Be prepared to present your ideas to the other members of your group.

1. Using the information in the article, create a timeline of 7–8 important dates and events in Fitzgerald's life on a separate sheet of paper.
2. Using the information speculate on the plot, the characters, themes and conflicts of *The Great Gatsby*.

 -

Speculating & predicting

Your task is to speculate on what the novel *The Great Gatsby* is about. Each member of your group focuses on a different set of information:

a) <u>the Jazz Age</u>, b) the author, c) some quotes, d) some stills from the movie.

Read your set of information on page 129/130 of your novel and complete the comprehension tasks given below. Be prepared to present your ideas to the other members of your group.

1. What is meant by the term "Jazz Age"? Make a mind-map illustrating its most important features.
2. The novel *The Great Gatsby* takes place and was written during the so-called Jazz Age. Speculate on its plot, setting, characters, possible themes and conflicts.

 -

Speculating & predicting

Your task is to speculate on what the novel *The Great Gatsby* is about. Each member of your group focuses on a different set of information:

a) the Jazz Age, b) the author, c) <u>some quotes</u>, d) some stills from the movie.

Read your set of information on the first pages of your novel ("Getting Started") and complete the comprehension tasks given below. Be prepared to present your ideas to the other members of your group.

1. What kind of novel do you believe *The Great Gatsby* is – a romance, a crime novel, a detective novel, a tragedy, a comedy, …? Why do you think so?
2. Based on your reading, speculate on the novel's plot, setting, characters, and possible themes and plots.

Speculating & predicting

Your task is to speculate on what the novel *The Great Gatsby* is about. Each member of your group focuses on a different set of information:

a) the Jazz Age,
b) the author,
c) some quotes,
d) <u>some stills from the movie</u>.

Read your set of information and complete the comprehension tasks given below.
Be prepared to present your ideas to the other members of your group.

1. What kind of novel do you believe *The Great Gatsby* is – a romance, a crime novel, a detective novel, a tragedy, a comedy, …? Why do you think so?
2. Based on your reading, speculate on the novel's plot, setting, characters, possible themes and plots.

Stills from the movie *The Great Gatsby* (1974)

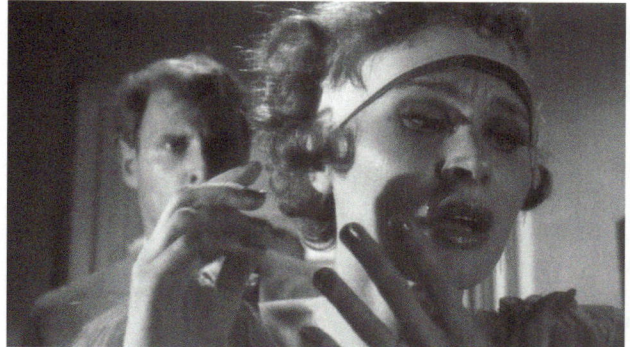 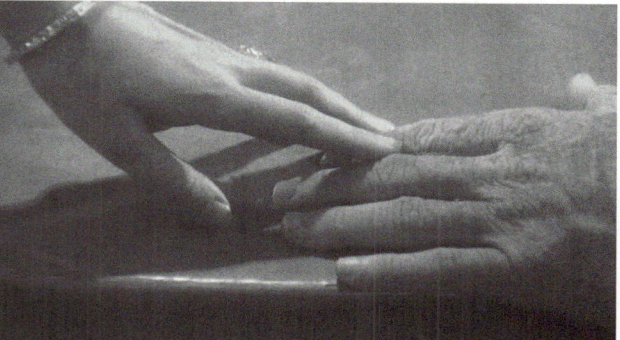

Literary terms to know: elements of fiction

When studying literature it is important to remember that a story consists of several elements: plot, characters, setting, point of view, conflict, theme. Different authors place different emphasis on any one or more of these elements. For instance, some authors may want the reader to focus on the plot, so the setting of the story may not be at the centre of attention. It is essential when analysing a piece of fiction that you look at all of the elements and how they work together to create an entire story.

Plot

- the sequence of events that make up a story
- exposition: the beginning of a story in which the main characters, conflicts, and setting are introduced.
- rising action: the action that takes place before the climax; the plot is complicated.
- turning point: marks a change (for better or worse) in the protagonist's affairs.
- climax: the highest point of tension or emotional peak for the protagonist.
- falling action: the action that takes place after the climax, leading to the resolution.
- resolution: the end of a story; problems are solved, and the characters' future may be foreshadowed.

Point of view

- the perspective from which the story is told
- narrator (the voice that tells the story) may or may not reflect the opinions and attitudes of the author himself/herself.
- first-person perspective: a narrator focuses on the thoughts, feelings, and opinions of a particular character.
- third-person limited perspective: a narrator observes the action as an outside observer, revealing the thoughts, feelings, and opinions of only one character.
- third-person omniscient perspective: a narrator that observes the action as an outside observer, however, revealing the thoughts, feelings, and opinions of several characters.

Conflict

- the struggle(s) between opposing forces, usually characters
- internal conflict: a character's struggle with himself/herself or his/her conscience.
- external conflict: a character's struggle with an outside force, such as another character, nature, or his/her environment.

Characters

- the individuals involved in the action of the story
- protagonist: the main character in a story
- antagonist: the conflicting force against the protagonist; can be another character, a force of nature, or the protagonist struggling against himself/herself.

Theme

- the main idea behind a piece of fiction, or message in the story

Setting

- the time and place, or where and when the action occurs

Speculating & predicting: group work

You are now familiar with the historical and biographical context of the novel you are about to read. In addition you gained some insight into the content by studying important quotes and stills taken from the film version.

As a group, complete the chart below with predictions about the novel *The Great Gatsby*. Remember, these are predictions, so there really are no wrong answers. However, you must use the knowledge you gained from the previous material to help you. Be sure to answer all the questions posed to you. An example has been given for you.

Remember to speak English at all times. Choose a presenter.

Literary elements	Predictions
Plot What do you predict the novel will be about? Give a 3–5 sentence summary of your ideas.	
Conflict What kinds of conflicts might the characters face? Include one internal and one external conflict that one of the characters may face.	
Characters What personality types will appear in the story? What do you think they might do for a living and for leisure? Choose two examples.	
Setting Where and when do you think the story might take place? Choose one example for each element.	*This story will very likely take place in the 1920s, during the Jazz Age. According to the article we read in class, this was a time of great prosperity. ...*
Theme What kinds of themes do you predict will be presented in this novel? Write out 3–5 themes in sentence form.	

Presentations

The Great Gatsby is set against the background of the 1920s, the so-called Roaring Twenties, or the Jazz Age. Life looked, felt, tasted, smelled and sounded totally different from today's world.

The following expressions are taken from the novel. Choose one, find out the exact meaning of the term and pick an illustration from the internet to help your classmates visualize the item. Be prepared to give a 20-second presentation on your choice.

People	Music & Fashion
• Midas	• Ain't We Got Fun
• Maecenas	• Mendelssohn Wedding March
• cadet	• Beale Street Blues
• Joe Friscoe	• bob
• Rockefeller	• pompadour
• Rosy Rosenthal	• crepe-de-Chine
• Trimalchio	
• El Greco	
• David Belasco	
• Gilda Gray	
• James J. Hill	

Places	Animals
• New Haven	• Airedale
• Long Island Sound	• beluga
• Lake Forest	• klipspringer
• Adam's study	• leech
• Queensboro Bridge	

Events	Literature
• the Great War	• Town Tattle
• World Series	• Simon Called Peter
• World's Fair	• Castel Rackrent
• World's Series transaction in 1919	• Hopalong Cassidy

Transportation	Drinking
• Dodge	• Prohibition
• Cunard, White Star Line	• bootlegger
	• Dewar
	• highballs

Understanding the time period – designing a stamp for the Jazz Age

The Great Gatsby takes place during the summer of 1922.

F. Scott Fitzgerald coined the phrase "the Jazz Age" that same year to describe the flamboyant "anything goes" period from 1918 to 1930, the years after World War I, continuing through the Twenties and ending with the rise of the Great Depression. This decade was both the gaudiest and saddest era in modern American history.

Imagine you are asked to design a stamp that represents that era. Together with your classmates research the time period and focus on the following aspects:

- Music and dancing (jazz and swing music, Charleston etc.)
- Fashion trends
- Prohibition (bootlegging, quickeasies)
- Changing role of women
- Black Friday and the Great Depression
- Political situation
- …

Together select an image that accurately symbolizes the time period.

Prepare an outline for a speech in front of the Citizen's Stamp Advisory Committee (the committee that decides on stamp designs) justifying why your stamp should be chosen to represent that decade.

Be prepared to present your design and hold your speech in front of the class. Remember to use *notes only*, to deliver your speech **freely** and at an **appropriate volume and speed**.

Useful structure and phrases:

Parts	Useful phrases (suggestions only)
Introduction • addressing the audience • topic/aim of your speech	Ladies and gentlemen, … We have gathered here to … It is an honour for me to be here today.
Main part • presentation of your model • reasons for your decision/design	I'd like to begin by …/Secondly … I'd like to move on to … Before we go any further, let's look at … Last but not least …
Conclusion • final remarks/thanking for attention	Let me conclude with … Thank you for listening so attentively! I do appreciate the chance to present our final design.

While-reading task: chapter 1

a) **Read chapter 1 of the novel. Then finish the following sentence beginnings. You may add sentences in between if you like:**

1. The narrator is a young Midwesterner who, having graduated from … in … and fought in …, has returned home to begin a career.

2. However, he feels … and in the year … he decides to move to … in order to …

3. He rents a house in …

4. The neighbouring house turns out to be …

5. One evening Nick is invited by … who lives in …

6. There he also meets …

7. When Tom Buchanan leaves to take a phone call, Jordan informs Nick that …

8. Tom makes no efforts to …

9. Before Nick leaves for West Egg, both Tom and Daisy encourage him to …

10. Upon returning home that evening, Nick notices …

11. While watching Gatsby, Nick witnesses a curious event: …

b) **The section can be divided into three parts:**

 * part I   p. 8: 16 to p. 10: 16
 * part II   p. 10: 17 to p. 20: 17
 * part III   p. 20: 18 to the end

Find a suitable title for each of the three parts of chapter 1.

_____

_____

_____

Component 2

Who is who? Characters and conflicts

2.1 Completing a character map

Da alle wesentlichen Charaktere und Konstellationen in den ersten beiden Kapiteln einge-führt werden, ist es für das weitere Verständnis des Romans sinnvoll, in einem ersten Bau-stein die verschiedenen Figuren genauer zu betrachten und ihre Beziehung zueinander zu erarbeiten. Die Verbindungen der Charaktere zueinander erscheinen auf den ersten Blick möglicherweise verwirrend, daher ist es hilfreich, die Konstellationen und Konfliktlinien op-tisch darstellen zu lassen, um den Schülerinnen und Schülern eine Orientierungshilfe für die weitere Lektüre an die Hand zu geben.

Die Grundlage für die Erstellung der *character map* bildet die vorbereitende Hausaufgabe *(Copy 6)*, die zu Beginn der Stunde verglichen werden sollte. Falls die Schülerinnen und Schüler beauftragt waren, das erste Kapitel in ihrem *reading log* zu dokumentieren, werden diese Ergebnisse besprochen und ggf. geklärt.

Lösungsvorschläge zu *Copy 6*

a)

1. The narrator is a young Midwesterner who, having graduated from Yale in 1915 and fought in World War I, has returned home to begin a career.

2. However, he feels restless and in the year 1922 he decides to move to New York City/to the East in order to become a successful bond salesman.

3. He rents a house in West Egg, Long Island.

4. The neighbouring mansion turns out to belong to Gatsby.

5. … by his cousin Daisy and her husband, Tom Buchanan, who live across the bay in the fashionable community of East Egg.

6. … Jordan Baker, a childhood friend of Daisy's and a professional golfer.

7. … Tom's mistress is on the phone.

8. … to cover up his affairs.

9. … go on a date with Jordan Baker.

10. … a figure emerging from Gatsby's mansion.

11. Gatsby, standing by the waterside, stretches his arms toward the darkness, trembling. However, Nick can only make out a green light in the distance, such as one that you find at the end of a dock across the Sound.

b)

- part I   The Narrator's Youth
- part II   At the Buchanans'
- part III The Green Light

Im Anschluss daran erhalten die Schülerinnen und Schüler den Auftrag, die Charaktere des ersten Kapitels und ihre Beziehungen zueinander visuell in einer *character map* darzustellen *(Copy 7)*. Diese Karte wird an dieser Stelle erst begonnen und muss Stück für Stück erweitert werden. Zur Orientierung können auch weitere Attribute hinzugefügt werden (e.g *profession, place of living*).

Lösungsvorschläge *character map*

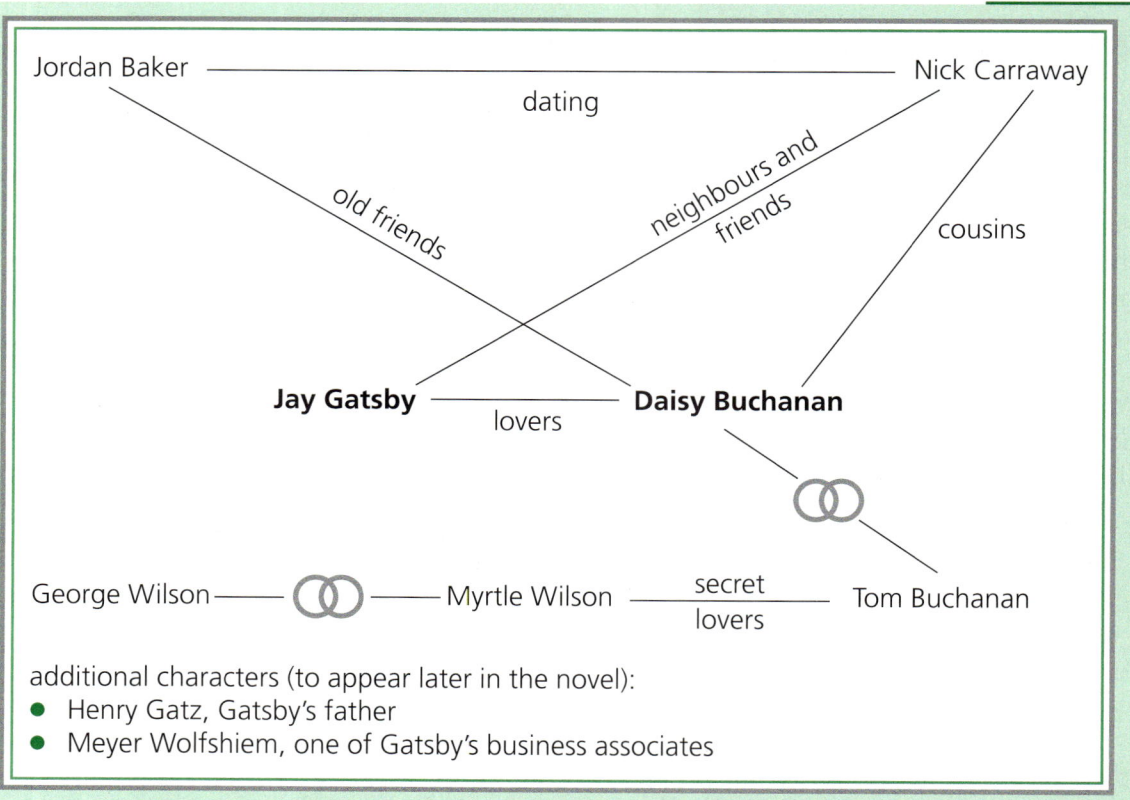

additional characters (to appear later in the novel):
- Henry Gatz, Gatsby's father
- Meyer Wolfshiem, one of Gatsby's business associates

2.2 Describing the characters (indirect and direct characterization)

Nachdem ein Orientierungsrahmen geschaffen wurde, werden nun in einem vertiefenden Schritt erste Charakteranalysen der Figuren erarbeitet.

Die Schülerinnen und Schüler sollen sich zunächst einen allgemeinen Überblick über die Möglichkeiten des Autors verschaffen, eine Figur zu charakterisieren (*direct and indirect characterization*). Ausgehend von den beiden folgenden eindeutigen Beispielen erkennen sie den Unterschied zwischen beiden Techniken, fiktionale Charaktere zu beschreiben.

Describe the differences between these two ways of describing a character:

Susan is a very eager and hard-working student. Lately, however, she is distracted by something, and she is not behaving like her usual self.	Lacy said, "Susan seems not to care about her school work anymore. It's as if she is distracted by or concerned about something. What do you think?" "I don't know, but it is certainly unlike her to get bad grades," Jennifer replied.

The author or narrator tells the reader what the character is like. ▶ direct characterization (or: telling technique)	The author gives information about a character and allows the reader to draw his/her own conclusions about that character. ▶ indirect characterization (or: showing technique)

Bevor die Schülerinnen und Schüler Beispiele für beide Techniken im Roman finden, um die Figuren zu charakterisieren, sollten noch weitere Strategien genannt werden, mit denen Figuren indirekt charakterisiert werden:

As can be seen in the example given above, the reader can make assumptions about a character by studying his/her interaction with other characters. Find additional ways to learn about a character in an indirect way.

The reader can draw conclusions about a character by studying his/her behaviour, his/her choice of words, his/her opinion, his/her way of talking etc.

Zur Vervollständigung werden im Unterrichtsgespräch die Aspekte herausgearbeitet, die für eine umfassende Charakterisierung wichtig sind. Die Ergebnisse werden in einem *cluster* gesammelt:

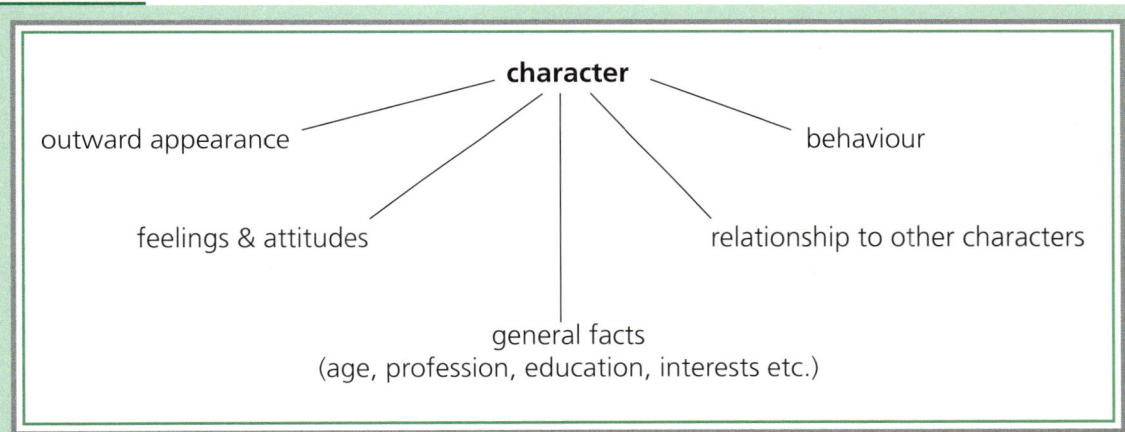

In einer anschließenden Anwendungsphase erhalten die Schülerinnen und Schüler die Aufgabe, sich auf eine Figur des ersten Kapitels zu konzentrieren und unter Berücksichtigung der oben entwickelten Verfahren zu beschreiben *(Copy 8)*. Die Schülerinnen und Schüler tauschen sich dann in Gruppen über die jeweiligen Figuren aus, sodass jedes Gruppenmitglied am Ende Informationen zu allen Charakteren hat.

Es bietet sich auch an, dass sich die Schüler gegenseitig überprüfen, d.h. sie präsentieren gegenseitig verschiedene Zitate und die anderen Gruppenmitglieder schließen auf den richtigen Charakter und analysieren die Textpassage hinsichtlich der Aussage über den Charakter sowie die Charakterisierungsmethode.

Diese Übung kann im Verlauf der Lektüre natürlich erweitert und wiederholt werden; dies gilt insbesondere für das zweite Kapitel, in dem zwei weitere wichtige Charaktere eingeführt werden (Ehepaar Wilson). Darüber hinaus entwickeln sich die Figuren im Verlauf des Romans entscheidend weiter, was dokumentiert werden sollte (siehe dazu unten: *long-term reading task*).

Lösungsvorschläge *Copy 8*

Daisy

direct	indirect
"low, thrilling voice" (12: 39)	"… but there was an excitement in her voice that men who cared for her found difficult to forget: a singing compulsion, a whispered "Listen," a promise that she had done gay, exciting things just a while since and there were gay, exciting things hovering in the next hour. …" (12: 43 ff.) = seductive
"Her face was sad and lovely with bright things in it, bright eyes and a bright passionate mouth, …" (12: 41 ff.)	
She has a three-year old daughter (13: 11 ff.)	Then she added irrelevantly: "You ought to see the baby." (13: 10 f.) = Daisy – a bad mother?
"Well, I've had a very bad time, Nick, and I'm pretty cynical about every-thing." (17: 40 f.)	"I'm glad it's a girl. And I hope she'll be a fool – that's the best thing a girl can be in this world, a beautiful little fool." (18: 9 ff.) = cynical, disappointed, hurt, aware of reality = she hopes that her daughter will be able to be blind to all the evil she has known; that she will be able to be beautiful enough to find herself a rich and handsome husband, but that she will not know about, or will be able to ignore his indiscretions.
She has an expression of unthoughtful sadness. (15: 18 f.)	
	"Hulking," insisted Daisy. (14: 39) = aggressive
	"I always watch for the longest day of the year and then I miss it." (14: 23 f.) = seeking for something
	"I'm p-paralyzed with happiness." (12: 23) "It's romantic, isn't it, Tom?" (17: 7 f.) = seemingly naive, foolish
	"I love to see you at my table, Nick. You remind me of a – of a rose, an absolute rose." (16: 16 f.) = flirtatious
	"You see I think everything's terrible anynow," she went on in a convinced way. "Everybody thinks so – the most advanced people. And I know. …" (18: 12 ff.) = pessimistic, disillusioned, grieving
	= ambivalent, vague, mysterious figure

Tom

direct	indirect
born somewhere in the Midwest, has lived in Chicago for some time; enormously wealthy family background; Yale graduate, successful American football player; current profession unknown, hobbies: horses, polo (10: 23 ff.)	"That's what I get for marrying a brute of a man, a great, big, hulking physical specimen of a ..." (14: 34 f.) = described by his wife Daisy as cruel, aggressive, bossy
has an affair with "some woman in New York" (16: 38 f.) "straw-haired man of 30 with a rather hard mouth and a supercilious manner", "two shining arrogant eyes", "enormous power of his body", "great pack of muscle", "a cruel body" (11: 8 ff.)	"I hate that word hulking," objected Tom crossly, "even in kidding." (14: 37 f.) = emotional, domineering verbal expression
"His speaking voice, of a gruff husky tenor, added to the impression of fractiousness he conveyed." (11: 18 f.)	"The idea is if we don't look out the white race will be – will be utterly submerged." (15: 15 ff.) = racist attitude, believes in the superiority of the white race and family values
	holds strong family values but has a secret love affair with another woman = hypocrite

Nick

direct	indirect
At the time *the story takes place* (around 1922) = as a character	
born in the Midwest, prominent background, well-to-do people who attribute their descendancy to the 'Dukes of Buccleuch'; graduated from Yale, participated in WWI, went to the East in 1922 to become a bond salesman, lived for about eight months in West Egg in a 'weather-beaten cardboard bungalow', hires a Finnish woman to keep the house. (8: 16 ff.)	capable of candid judgements when he says that Daisy should leave Tom at once. (20: 10 f.)
restless after end of WWI (8: 27 ff.)	He considers himself "a guide, a path-finder, an original settler" (9: 10 f.) = he wants to explore the East and its urban civilization
disillusioned and frustrated with the provincialism of the Midwest (8: 29 ff.)	"And I had the high intention of reading many other books besides. ..." (9: 23 ff.) = well-read, well-educated, fascinated by wealth and the very rich.
At the time he *narrates the story* = as the narrator	
	When he was younger he was more "vulnerable" (7: 1) = he is less easily influenced now
	He listens to his father's advice (7: 1) = he is respectful, obedient?
	He is "inclined to reserve all judgements" (7: 7 f.) = he is tolerant, open-minded, does not jump to conclusions
	He was "privy to the secret griefs" of people (7: 14 f.) = people confided in him

He believes that "reserving judgements is a matter of infinite hope" (7: 21 f.)
= tolerance towards others is something positive, one should respect the ideas and feelings of others

He believes that "a sense of the fundamental decencies is parcelled out unequally at birth" (7: 24 f.)
= he is aware of the fact that he is privileged

Jordan

direct	indirect
physical attributes: sporty, athletic figure, slender, small-breasted, erect carriage, grey sun-strained eyes; (13: 45 ff.) professional golf champion (18: 41 ff.)	"wan, charming, discontented face" (14: 4 ff.) = arrogant, self-sufficient, curious, discontented "… I had heard some story of her too, a critical, unpleasant story, but …" (19: 5 ff.) = mysterious woman

Jay Gatsby

direct	indirect
owner of a very expensive, unique mansion (10: 3 ff.)	description of house (10: 3 ff.) = tasteless figure?, he possibly wants to show off his new wealth "You must know Gatsby." (14: 10) = apparently well-known in New York City (what for?) "stretched out his arms toward the dark water in a curious way … he was trembling." (20: 37 ff.) and "When I looked once more … he had vanished." (20: 42) = mysterious, ghostlike, isolated, lonely versus: "his leisurely movements … and the secure position of his feet upon the lawn" (20: 30 f.) = self-confident, calm = ambivalent figure

Abschließend bieten sich verschiedene kreative Schreibaufträge an, bei denen die Schülerinnen und Schüler die verschiedenen Einzelergebnisse berücksichtigen müssen.

- How do you expect the story to continue? Write down a brief plot outline that includes at least two plausible conflicts to be resolved at the end of the story.

- The next day, Daisy meets her cousin Nick again. This time they can be more personal and Daisy starts talking about her life with Tom. What does she say? How does Nick react? Write down their conversation.

  She complains about her husband's affairs, his racist attitudes, his aggressiveness and dominance; Nick probably urges her to leave him immediately. Or:
  She might cover up her problems and try to distract Nick from her apparent unhappiness and frustration; tries to involve him in a different conversation.

- Read your notes about the characters again and make personal notes about them by completing the following sentences:
  I like the way …   I am unhappy about …
  I dislike the way …   I am pleased about …
  I think …   I am confused about …
  I don't believe …   I am convinced that …
  Give evidence from the text to support your opinion.

- long-term reading task: designing a bookmark

Für den weiteren Verlauf der Lektüre wählen die Schülerinnen und Schüler eine Figur aus, auf die sie ihr Augenmerk ganz besonders richten, sie sozusagen „detektivisch" begleiten ("shadowing") und ihre Persönlichkeitsentwicklung beobachten.
Folgender Arbeitsauftrag wird den Schülern nach der gemeinsamen Erarbeitung der ersten beiden Kapitel präsentiert:

- Choose one of the characters introduced in the first two chapters of the novel.
- In order to increase your understanding of the character complete the following tasks as you continue reading *The Great Gatsby*:
  - Find a picture or a photograph that you think could represent your character. You may use magazines, newspapers, advertisements etc.
  - Turn your picture into a bookmark and write a brief description of your character on the backside of it. As you learn more about the character throughout the work, add to that description.

2.3 Analysing the point of view

Der Roman zeichnet sich hinsichtlich des Erzählers durch eine Besonderheit aus: Nick Carraway ist der Ich-Erzähler, gleichzeitig aber auch eine Figur der Handlung (erzählender und erlebender Ich-Erzähler). Im ersten Abschnitt des ersten Kapitels stellt sich der Ich-Erzähler selbst vor und erläutert die Erzählsituation: Er erzählt eine bereits vergangene Geschichte, die sich um das Jahr 1922 zugetragen hat, und bewertet das Geschehen bereits in der Einleitung.
Bevor die Schülerinnen und Schüler sich mit dem Erzähler Nick Carraway auseinandersetzen, erfolgt zunächst eine Wiederholung wichtiger Erzählperspektiven, ihrer Funktion und Wirkung auf den Leser. Dazu studieren die Schülerinnen und Schüler den Informationstext

auf Seite 132/133 der Romanausgabe und erhalten den Auftrag, die beiden Hauptperspektiven (*first-person* und *third-person narrative perspective*) in ihren verschiedenen Eigenschaften und Funktionen visuell darzustellen.

Vertiefend äußern sich die Schülerinnen und Schüler kritisch zu der Verlässlichkeit der Erzähler:

> Which narrator would you trust the least/the most?

Nun kann die Überleitung zu dem ersten Abschnitt des Romans erfolgen:

> Who is the narrator in the novel *The Great Gatsby?*
>
> First-person narrator named Nick Carraway

Nun lesen die Schülerinnen und Schüler erstmals die *opening paragraphs* des ersten Kapitels unter folgender Fragestellung, die das Grobverständnis sichern soll:

> Read the opening paragraphs of the first chapter of our novel. Pay special attention to the aspect of time and place: *When* does Nick Carraway express his thoughts? *Where* is he as he narrates the first paragraphs of this chapter? Complete the diagram.

Folgendes Diagramm wird an der Tafel/auf OH-Folie präsentiert, das die Schülerinnen und Schüler nach der Lektüre vervollständigen (die Überschriften, die sich auf den bereits erarbeiteten Teil des ersten Kapitels beziehen, sollten von den Schülerinnen und Schülern stammen, s. *Copy 6*).

Narrative structure of the novel

narrator's youth in the Midwest/ his moving to West Egg ⟶ dinner at the Buchanans' (1922) ⟶ the Green Light/ meeting Mr Gatsby

↓

narrator is in the Midwest (again), some time after 1922

= It becomes clear that Nick Carraway speaks in the (fictional) present, narrating a story from memory that took place in the past (1922).

Um die neuen, sprachlich anspruchsvollen Informationen über den Erzähler sowie die Funktion der Einleitung zu erkennen, bearbeiten die Schülerinnen und Schüler *Copy 9*, die den Schülerinnen und Schülern ausreichend Hilfestellung bietet.

Lösungsvorschläge *Copy 9*

QUOTES	
1. "In my younger and more vulnerable years my father gave me some advice that I've been turning over in my mind ever since. 'Whenever you feel like criticizing anyone,' he told me, 'just remember that all the people in his world haven't had the advantages that you've had." (7: 1 ff.)	he respects his father; before judging someone he should remember the many privileges he has enjoyed

2. "In consequence, I'm inclined to reserve all judgments, a habit that has opened up many curious natures to me and also made me the victim of not a few veteran bores." (7: 8ff.)	he tries to keep an open mind
3. "Reserving judgment is a matter of infinite hope." (7: 21f.)	tolerance gives people the chance to develop into better people; tolerance towards others is something positive
4. "I was privy to the secret griefs of wild, un-known men." (7: 14f.)	people confided in him
5. "[A] sense of the fundamental decencies is parcelled out unequally at birth." (7: 24f.)	he is aware of his natural superiority; a tolerant attitude is a natural privilege, not something one can acquire at will –
6. "And, after boasting this way of my tolerance, I come to the admission that it has a limit. Conduct may be founded on the hard rock or the wet marshes, but after a certain point I don't care what it's founded on." (7: 26ff.)	there are, however, limits to his tolerance
7. "Only Gatsby, the man who gives his name to this book, was exempt from my reaction – Gats-by, who represented everything for which I have an unaffected scorn." (7: 33ff.)	Gatsby is exempted from his harsh condemnation
8. "... there was something gorgeous about him, some heightened sensitivity to the promises of life ... it was an extraordinary gift for hope, a romantic readiness such as I have never found in any other person ..." (8: 4ff.)	he admires Gatsby for certain qualities even though he also criticizes him (contrast statement 7 vs. 8)

Vertiefend wird die besondere Rolle des Erzählers im Roman diskutiert:

Why does Nick narrate the story of Gatsby?

His primary motive for narrating the story is to tell something about the events which changed his opinion on the notion of tolerance (how his own father taught him to believe). This change of mind ultimately made him leave the East, full of disappointment.

What are the disadvantages and advantages of having Nick narrate the story of *The Great Gatsby*, rather than having Gatsby tell the story himself?

advantages:
Nick gives a more objective view of all the characters in the novel; the reader wants to find out more about Gatsby because Nick does = realistic approach; Nick is able to point out subtle nuances about Gatsby that the reader might not otherwise get (if Gatsby had told the story).

disadvantages:
Nick is not a neutral observer but quite capable of severe judgments (e.g. comment on Daisy's marriage at the end of ch. 1); he openly expresses his admiration for Gatsby (see opening paragraphs) and therefore he will be far from objective with respect to this person.

Read and respond

Thematisch kann der Aspekt der Toleranz, von der der Erzähler sehr stolz berichtet, von den Schülerinnen und Schülern diskutiert werden. Folgende *writing prompts* eignen sich für Einträge in die *reading journals* (oder für mündliche Partnerarbeit):

> "And after boasting this way of my tolerance, I come to the admission that it has a limit."
> Define 'tolerance' and/or 'intolerance' in your own words. Describe a situation in which you or someone you know showed tolerance and/or intolerance. Is intolerance prevalent in our society today? In a paragraph, give some examples.

Als vorbereitende Hausaufgabe lesen die Schülerinnen und Schüler das zweite Kapitel und bearbeiten *Copy 10*.

2.4 Describing and analysing the setting I (chapter 2)

Die ersten beiden Kapitel des Romans sind nicht nur deshalb wichtig, weil sie alle wesentlichen Figuren und Konfliktlinien vorstellen, sondern weil sie ebenfalls eine genaue Beschreibung der Handlungsorte beinhalten, die im Roman nicht rein zufällig auftauchen. Vielmehr tragen alle genannten Orte eine symbolische Bedeutung: Bestimmte Werte und Qualitäten sind mit den Handlungsorten und den dort lebenden Charakteren verbunden ('moral geography').

Im zweiten Kapitel werden zwei neue Handlungsorte (Valley of Ashes und New York) und mit den Wilsons zwei wichtige Nebenfiguren eingeführt. Durch die genaue Beschreibung der Orte und ihrer Repräsentanten wird schnell deutlich, dass das zweite Kapitel einen eindrucksvollen Kontrast zum ersten und auch dritten Kapitel bildet.

Um das Zusammenspiel von Charakteren, Handlung und Schauplätzen herauszuarbeiten, muss zunächst eine (kurze) Personenbeschreibung der neuen Figuren (im Kontrast zu den Figuren des ersten Kapitels) erfolgen, bevor die Eigenschaften dann in einem zweiten Schritt auf die *settings* übertragen werden können. In leistungsstärkeren Kursen können die folgenden Aufgaben zur Charakterisierung auch begleitend zur Lektüre des zweiten Kapitels bearbeitet werden.

Der Einstieg erfolgt über das Bild *(Copy 11)*, das die Schüler auf der Grundlage ihrer Hausaufgabe erläutern sollen.

Lösungsvorschläge *Copy 10*

Folgende Sätze beziehen sich auf Kapitel 2 (in chronologischer Reihenfolge):

1. The Valley of Ashes is described as a desolate wasteland halfway between West Egg and New York.

2. Tom Buchanan takes Nick to George Wilson's garage, which lies at the edge of the Valley of Ashes.

3. Wilson's wife, Myrtle, is the woman with whom Tom has been having an affair.

4. Tom forces both Myrtle and Nick to accompany him to the city.

5. There, in the flat in which Tom pursues his affair, they have a shrill, vulgar party with Myrtle's sister, Catherine, and a repulsive couple named McKee.

6. The group gossips about Jay Gatsby: Catherine claims that he is somehow related to Kaiser Wilhelm, the much-despised ruler of Germany during World War I.

7. The group becomes exceedingly drunk; as a result, Myrtle begins to grow garrulous and harsh.

8. Tom tells her that she has no right to say Daisy's name.

9. Shortly after Tom gives her a puppy as a gift, Myrtle begins chanting Daisy's name to irritate Tom.

10. She continues taunting him, and he responds by breaking Myrtle's nose.

Sentences 8 and 12 do not refer to chapter 2.

Zur Charakterisierung der Wilsons erhalten die Schülerinnen und Schüler folgende Arbeitsaufträge:

1. Reread the following quotations from chapter 2 about Myrtle Wilson. Match each quotation with a suitable general quality of this character. Be prepared to explain your choices.

    Lösungsvorschläge:

p. 22: 34 – p. 23: 12	ugly, cheap, vulgar, seductive, coarse – sensuous
p. 23: 27 – p. 24: 19	pathetic: tries to become a part of the exclusive world of the Buchanans
p. 24: 37 – 40	pathetic: tries to become a part of the exclusive world of the Buchanans
p. 26: 8 – 23	spurious, fake, cheap: tries ambitiously to become the image she has of a member of a higher social class
p. 27: 7 – 13	pathetic: tries hard to adopt the manners of a society hostess
p. 30: 7 – 14	fake, pathetic: tries to live on a grand scale

    general qualities:
    sensuous – vulgar – cheap – pathetic – ugly – coarse – spurious – strident – funny – comical – ludicrous

2. Produce your own matching exercise based on George Wilson for another group/pair of students.

    Lösungsvorschläge:

p. 22: 15 – p. 23: 12	without energy or courage; weak man; a failure; submissive; useless; hopeless;

Abschließend diskutieren die Schülerinnen und Schüler folgende Fragen:

Why do you think Tom is attracted to Myrtle? Why does he not leave Daisy?

Myrtle is the opposite of Daisy. He may be attracted to Myrthe because she is loud and bawdy and does not really allow him to push her around (for the most part). He may just also like her because she is different and he finds the whole affair exciting. He does not want a divorce because he probably just enjoys the danger and game of the affair (and to boost his ego).

Für die Beschreibung und Analyse der Schauplätze erhalten die Schülerinnen und Schüler als Orientierungshilfe eine übersichtliche Karte der Region, auf der sie zunächst nach der Lektüre der ersten beiden Kapitel die vier wesentlichen Orte lokalisieren und ihnen die verschiedenen Personengruppen zuordnen *(Copy 12)*. Die detaillierte Textarbeit kann dann in arbeitsteiliger Gruppenarbeit erfolgen, sodass sich Experten für die jeweiligen Orte finden, die ihren Mitschülern ihre Ergebnisse im Anschluss präsentieren.

Im weiteren Verlauf der Unterrichtsarbeit wird die Tabelle dann immer weiter ergänzt (gilt insbesondere für den Handlungsort New York City sowie die Frage nach der symbolischen Bedeutung der Orte).

Folgende Aspekte sollen im Laufe der Unterrichtsarbeit eingetragen werden:

Setting	Characters	Description/events	Reflection of characters
West Egg	Nick, Gatsby	events: Gatsby's parties, Nick moves here; Nick sees Gatsby holding out his arms towards the green light at the end of the dock Gatsby's mansion: a 'colossal affair by any standard' (10: 6/7); a 'factual imitation of some …' (10: 7ff); marble swimming-pool = pretentious, huge, tasteless, flashy, fake, needs status symbol to display wealth = contrast to fashionable East Egg Nick's bungalow: meagre, simple bungalow between two 'newly wealthy' homes;	Nick: setting underlines Nick's simple, common, friendly personality Gatsby: mansion illustrates his aim to impress and awe visitors
East Egg	Daisy & Tom Buchanan Jordan Baker	events: Nick reunites with the Buchanans; Nick meets Jordan; the reader finds out about Tom's love affair. description: 'white palaces of fashionable East Egg glittered …' (10: 17); 'elaborate house' (10: 43); 'cheerful red-and-white Georgian Colonial mansion' (10:43ff); 'glowing with reflected gold' (11: 5); 'the windows were gleaming white' (11: 40). = elegant and airy Georgian Colonial mansion oozing with a hint of old memory = fashionable, wealthy, elite, tasteful, glamorous, pleasant atmosphere	Buchanans: home reflects their elite and wealthy background (family possessing inherited wealth)

Setting	Characters	Description/events	Reflection of characters
Valley of Ashes	Myrtle & Tom Wilson	events: Nick meets George and Myrtle; Tom shows off Myrtle and takes her to New York. description: located between West Egg and New York City; includes Wilson's garage, famous sign of Dr. T.J. Eckleburg; run-down, dusty, dismal unprosperous, ashen apartment above a garage 'a fantastic farm where ashes grow like wheat into ridges and hills and grotesque gardens; where ashes take the form of houses … of ash-gray men who move dimly … a line of gray cars crawls along … gives out a ghastly creak' (21: 4 ff.) = desolate, grim, meaningless, grotesque wasteland, dump land	Wilsons: setting underlines their grey and desolate situation; being a victim of the rich; submission George is indistinguishable from his surroundings; he has no personality of his own
New York City	Myrtle Wilson/Tom party guests later in the novel: Wolfshiem	events: party in Myrtle's apartment where Tom takes Nick to as well includes Myrtle's apartment rented by Tom (later: the Plaza Hotel, the restaurant) vulgar party; clear contrast to Buchanans' dinner party (ch. 1)	party guests (especially Myrtle): cheap, vulgar, pathetic place where the two worlds meet (West and East Egg)

Als Vertiefung ordnen die Schülerinnen und Schüler den Handlungsorten passende Werte zu, die durch die *settings* und ihre Bewohner symbolisiert werden. Diese können dann in die Karte eingetragen werden.

> It is often argued that the novel is based on a so-called 'moral geography'. Certain settings represent specific values. In your opinion, which general values do the places symbolize? Write down your ideas by labelling your map in different colours. One example has been done for you:
> Valley of Ashes = represents the plight of the poor, decay …

Lösungsvorschläge *Copy 12*

West Egg = symbolizes the superficial world of the newly rich (nouveau riche) with bad taste

East Egg = represents the hollowness and carelessness of the upper class (?)
colour white: may symbolize innocence, purity, high ideals but also coldness, sterility
colour deep red: may symbolize sadness, melancholy, death (?)
gold: symbolizes money and wealth

Valley of

Ashes = symbolizes desolation, decay, lives of the victims of society/the rich; represents the plight of the poor; submission; world of the working poor; dependency on the rich

New York = represents money and pleasure; corruption (Wolfshiem)

Abschließend bearbeiten die Schülerinnen und Schüler einen der beiden kreativen Schreibaufträge von *Copy 12*.

Read and respond

"I'm going to make a list of all the things I've got to get. A massage and a wave, and a collar for the dog, and one of those little ash-trays where you touch a spring, and a wreath with a black silk bow for mother's grave that'll last all summer. I got to write down a list so I won't forget all the things I got to do." (Myrtle Wilson, ch. 2, 30: 7 ff.)

How do you define "luxury" or having a luxurious life style? What does it include? Do you or someone you know live in luxury? How important is it for you, your family, your friends? What are advantages or disadvantages of a luxurious life style? In a paragraph, write what you think.

2.5 Describing and analysing the setting II: Gatsby and his parties (chapter 3)

Lösungsvorschläge *Copy 13*

a) 1. true, 2. false (Gatsby keeps aloof from his own party), 3. false (Caterers deliver the delicious food for the party), 4. false (They were a curious mixture of guests), 5. true, 6. true, 7. false (They were uninvited guests), 8. false (They mixed and changed places all the time), 9. false (It is one of many rumours that he hears about Gatsby), 10. true.

Im Vordergrund des dritten Kapitels steht die spektakuläre Sommerparty Gatsbys, auf der Nick – wie der Leser auch – zum ersten Mal persönlich auf Jay Gatsby trifft. Die ausführliche Darstellung der Party hat in erster Linie die Funktion, Gatsby zu charakterisieren, sodass dies im Mittelpunkt der nun vorgestellten Unterrichtsvorschläge steht. Es bietet sich an, die extensive Gästeliste am Anfang des vierten Kapitels miteinzubeziehen (als zusätzliches Mittel zur Charakterisierung der typischen Gäste einer typischen Gatsby-Party).
Als Einstieg in die Stunde sammeln die Schülerinnen und Schüler Beispiele für eine gelungene Party:

What makes a good party?

In einem *close-reading* erarbeiten die Schülerinnen und Schüler verschiedene Textpassagen und untersuchen Merkmale des Schauplatzes, der Charaktere und ihres Verhaltens *(Copy 14)*. Im Anschluss erstellen die Schülerinnen und Schüler einen sogenannten ,*fun-graph*', der den Grad und Verlauf des Vergnügens visuell darstellt (s. Aufgabe 2, *Copy 14*).

Die relevanten Textpassagen können in Partner- oder Gruppenarbeit erarbeitet werden:

> p. 32: 1–37: 27
> p. 39: 13–41: 7
> p. 41: 44–43: 25
> p. 46: 1–47: 36 (opening paragraphs of ch. 4)

Folgende Eigenschaften sollten in der Analyse der Party-Beschreibung genannt und können auf Folie gesammelt werden:

> setting:
> - music through the summer nights
> - the buffet tables "garnished with glistening hors d'œuvre, spiced baked …" (p. 32: 23–30)
> - the coloured lights that made a "Christmas tree of Gatsby's enormous garden" (p. 32: 22f.)
> - "the halls and salons and verandas are gaudy with primary colours, and hair bobbed in strange new ways, and shawls beyond the dreams of Castile" (p. 32: 36–38)
> - "floating rounds of cocktail permeate the garden outside" (32: 39)
> = an incredible lavishness, a magnificent display of luxury, an air of unbridled consumption; much alcohol, waste
>
> guests:
> - people moved "like moths among the whisperings and the champagne and the stars" (p. 32: 2–4) = attracted by a bright light
> - toward the end of the party, people are getting more and more drunk, "most of the remaining women" are having fights "with men said to be their husbands", because they are reluctant to leave. (p. 40: 30–38)
> - arrive in their Rolls Royce (= symbol of exclusiveness)
> - variety of people: elderly men, chorus girls, a group of young Englishmen, married couples, …
> - their behaviour: they perform "stunts all over the garden", girls dance by themselves, take musical instruments from the orchestra etc.
>   = diverse, no selection, uninvited, no relationship to host; unrestrained and eccentric behaviour
> - list of names: many names have to do with animals and plants; are connected with strange incidents, fatal accidents or suicide; or are connected with the fashionable world of the movie and the theatre. Possible functions of curious mixture: to show the absence of the normal; to show that many of Gatsby's guests have no family background but follow, like animals, only their desire for sex, money, and success.
>
> general character of the event:
> at the beginning: "amusement park" (p. 33: 28), hilarious and gay mood,
> → changes to …
> sudden emptiness at the end, fighting between people, bizarre accident; sole aim of the party is having fun, general lack of real social contact ('but the girls had moved casually on and her remark was addressed to the premature moon')

Nach der Präsentation der Schülerprodukte bietet es sich an, einen Ausschnitt der tatsächlichen filmischen Umsetzung gemeinsam zu sehen und Unterschiede bzw. Gemeinsamkeiten zu vergleichen und die Ergebnisse insgesamt zu bewerten.

Wie im nächsten Unterrichtsschritt deutlich wird, hat die ausführliche Darstellung von Gatsbys Party vor allem die Funktion, die Figur Gatsby zu beschreiben. Darüber hinaus ist der Roman aber auch ein Spiegelbild von einem gesellschaftlichen Ausschnitt der USA der Zwanzigerjahre. Falls noch nicht erfolgt, kann nun der Informationstext über das *Jazz Age* (s. S. 129 der Textausgabe) zum Einsatz kommen, um die Verbindung zu erklären. Nachdem wesentliche Merkmale der Epoche erarbeitet wurden, sind folgende Arbeitsaufträge denkbar:

1. **What parallels do you see between society as depicted in the information text and Gatsby's guests?**

   Alcohol, cars, lack of moral and behavioural standards, fashionable girls, bond business, sheer abundance of everything are important elements of Gatsby's parties and reflect the crass materialism of the 1920s among certain social groups. Attending a party where alcohol flowed freely implied a total rejection of the law and of American values. It also meant turning a blind eye to all the criminal activities connected with the production and distribution of alcohol.

2. **Based on what you know about the *Jazz Age* and your analysis of Gatsby's party explain the following proverb:**

   Life may not be the party we hoped for, but while we're here we should dance.

In einem zweiten Schritt kann nun der Rückschluss auf Gatsbys Charakter gezogen werden.

After looking at his parties, describe the host, Jay Gatsby. Choose five adjectives that describe his personality.

Die Ideen werden gesammelt und den drei Kategorien ‚positive', ‚negative' und ‚mysterious' zugeordnet.

Lösungsvorschläge

Positive	Negative	Mysterious
generous hospitable modern liberal polite, considerate engaging smile elegant	rumours mentioned by some of the guests (e.g. Gatsby killed sb., relative of the German Kaiser) lavish life style shallow superficial tasteless fake (huge library, remarks by Owl Eyes in the library scene) too formal dishonest (accusation by Jordan) lonely, isolated (keeps himself aloof from his guests)	does not attend his own parties seemingly without a past two strange phone calls (one well after 2am) = indirect suggestions of shady dealings? Nick receives the only formal invitation

= overall conclusion: ambivalent figure, "stage director of his own show"

Auf der Basis der Übersicht spekulieren die Schülerinnen und Schüler nun über die Gründe
für Gatsbys spektakuläre Partys:

 What could be the true reason for his extravagant parties if Gatsby does not
seem to really attend and enjoy them?

Character map

Nick Carraway

Tom Buchanan

Daisy Buchanan

Myrtle Wilson

Jay Gatsby

Jordan Baker

George Wilson

Describing characters

Choose one of the following characters and complete the chart with textual examples of both direct and indirect characterization from chapter 1 of the novel. Explain how and why your examples reveal something about the character. For further ideas, you may want to look at the box of useful adjectives given at the bottom of the page. Do not forget to give reference from the text (page & line). You can also take into account the film stills on page 52. One example has been done for you:

Character: Tom Buchanan	
Direct characterization (… what the narrator says)	"He was a sturdy straw-haired man of thirty with a rather hard mouth and a supercilious manner …" (p. 11: 8 ff.)
Indirect characterization (… what other characters say indirectly)	"It's up to us, who are the dominate race, to watch out or these other races will have control of things." (p. 15: 23 f.)
What is revealed?	arrogant, bossy, dominant man; racist attitudes, feels superior

Character:	
Direct characterization (… what the narrator says)	
Indirect characterization (… what other characters say indirectly)	
What is revealed?	

Useful adjectives:

intelligent/stupid ■ old/young ■ strong/weak ■ energetic/lazy ■ honest/dishonest ■ humourless/ good-humoured ■ quiet/talkative ■ cynical/naive ■ submissive/dominant ■ optimistic/pessimistic ■ secretive ■ vain ■ humble ■ mean ■ fair ■ articulate ■ hypocritical ■ superficial ■ trustworthy ■ agile/slow moving ■ apathetic ■ pathetic …

Nick Carraway – the ideal narrator?

The Great Gatsby is told from the first person point of view and by narrator Nick Carraway. The following excerpts are taken from the opening paragraphs in which Nick introduces himself. What can you infer from these passages about his character and personality?

His language is quite complicated and complex though. Match the following attributes to the corresponding quotes.

> Gatsby is exempted from his harsh condemnation ■ he is aware of his natural superiority ■ a tolerant attitude is a natural privilege, not something one can acquire at will ■ tolerance towards others is something positive ■ people confided in him ■ he admires Gatsby for certain qualities even though he also criticizes him ■ tolerance gives people the chance to develop into better persons ■ there are, however, limits to his tolerance ■ he respects his father ■ he tries to keep an open mind ■ before judging someone he should remember the many privileges he has enjoyed

Quotes	
1. "In my younger and more vulnerable years my father gave me some advice that I've been turning over in my mind ever since. 'Whenever you feel like criticizing anyone,' he told me, 'just remember that all the people in his world haven't had the advantages that you've had." (7: 1 ff.)	
2. "In consequence, I'm inclined to reserve all judgments, a habit that has opened up many curious natures to me and also made me the victim of not a few veteran bores." (7: 8 ff.)	
3. "Reserving judgment is a matter of infinite hope." (7: 21 f.)	
4. "I was privy to the secret griefs of wild, unknown men." (7: 14 f.)	
5. "A sense of the fundamental decencies is parceled out unequally at birth." (7: 24 f.)	
6. "And, after boasting this way of my tolerance, I come to the admission that it has a limit. Conduct may be founded on the hard rock or the wet marshes, but after a certain point I don't care what it's founded on." (7: 26 f.)	
7. "Only Gatsby, the man who gives his name to this book, was exempt from my reaction – Gatsby, who represented everything for which I have an unaffected scorn." (7: 33 ff.)	
8. "... there was something gorgeous about him, some heightened sensitivity to the promises of life ... it was an extraordinary gift for hope, a romantic readiness such as I have never found in any other person ..." (8: 4 ff.)	

While-reading task: chapter 2

a) **Here is a list of 12 events and statements. Only ten of them refer to chapter 2. Choose the right ten and put them in the correct order.**

1. The group becomes exceedingly drunk; as a result, Myrtle begins to grow garrulous and harsh.

2. Tom tells her that she has no right to say Daisy's name.

3. Shortly after Tom gives her a puppy as a gift, Myrtle begins chanting Daisy's name to irritate Tom.

4. Tom Buchanan takes Nick to George Wilson's garage, which lies at the edge of the Valley of Ashes.

5. The Valley of Ashes is described as a desolate wasteland halfway between West Egg and New York.

6. She continues taunting him, and he responds by breaking Myrtle's nose.

7. Wilson's wife, Myrtle, is the woman with whom Tom has been having an affair.

8. Tom explains that he cannot leave Daisy because of their little daughter.

9. Tom forces both Myrtle and Nick to accompany him to the city.

10. There, in the flat in which Tom pursues his affair, they have a shrill, vulgar party with Myrtle's sister, Catherine, and a repulsive couple named McKee.

11. The group gossips about Jay Gatsby: Catherine claims that he is somehow related to Kaiser Wilhelm, the much-despised ruler of Germany during World War I.

12. George tells Myrtle that he is going to sell the garage and move to the West.

b) **Find a suitable title for chapter 2.**

Partying in New York City

This still is taken from the film *The Great Gatsby* (1974). Based on your reading, give plausible answers to the following questions:

1. Where does the action take place?

2. Who are the two people in the still and why is the woman's nose bleeding?

Know the place!

Places in *The Great Gatsby* are not just geographical sites where people just happen to live. The four different settings are rather important, because in Fitzgerald's world, setting reveals character and represents certain values, or the lack thereof. Fitzgerald divides the world into four major settings: East Egg, West Egg, the Valley of Ashes, and New York City.

Take a look at the map and mark the four settings using different colours. Based on your reading of chapter 1 and 2 make notes on the following questions:

- Who lives in the four different settings?
- What are typical features of the settings?
- What important events have taken place so far?
- How does each home reflect the personality of its owners?

The expressions given below may be helpful. Make sure you give evidence from the novel to support your ideas.

glamorous ■ desolate ■ fashionable ■ tasteless ■ cheap ■ beautiful ■ depressing ■ fake ■ huge ■ vulgar ■ desolate ■ rural ■ grim ■ dim ■ exciting ■ pleasant ■ cosmopolitan ■ boring ■ meagre ■ ostentatious ■ showy ■ elegant ■ airy ■ bare ■ run-down ■ prosperous

Writing tasks

1. Choose one of the settings you have just described. What sort of story do you think will take place in this particular setting?

2. Imagine you worked as an estate agent and you had to sell a house built in one of the places you have just described. Produce a 'For Sale' advertisement for this property. Before you start, think about your potential clients (who would such a property appeal to?) and how you could address them. Play down any negative sides of the place and accentuate the positive ones.

While-reading task: chapter 3

a) **Read the first half of chapter 3 and decide whether the following statements are true or false. Rewrite the false ones.**

1. Gatsby's parties always started at dusk.

2. Gatsby stood at the door to greet guests as they arrived.

3. The food was all prepared by Gatsby's own cook in his kitchens.

4. All guests knew each other before the party.

5. There was a very large orchestra to play music at the parties.

6. The guests wore bright colours and the most fashionable clothes and hairdos.

7. All of Gatsby's guests had to show invitation cards at the door before they were allowed to enter the party.

8. The guests tended to stay in their own little groups all evening.

9. Nick finds out that his neighbour has German ancestors.

10. The party became very noisy as the evening wore on.

b) **Write five more true or false statements about the second half of this chapter. Write down the corrected version of your false statements.**

_____

_____

_____

_____

_____

c) **Find a suitable title for this chapter. What is the defining event? What are the most important people and/or themes?**

_____

Ain't we got fun?!

Every weekend, hundreds of people attend the famous summer parties at Gatsby's mansion in West Egg. What make them so incredibly popular, special and glamorous?

1. Reread the description of the party closely. Make notes on the following aspects:

Who are the guests? What do they do?	What does the location look like?
How do the guests behave?	**What is the general aim of the event, the motivation of the guests to attend the event?**

Do not forget to give evidence from the text.

2. Imagine you were a guest at the party. Describe the level of fun or excitement you would experience during that particular night by completing a 'fun graph': The vertical line shows the level of fun on a scale of 10 points. The horizontal line refers to the time aspect (beginning – end of the party). Be prepared to give evidence from the text to support your ideas.

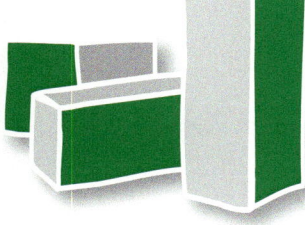

A dream has come true?

3.1 Foreshadowing and predicting (chapter 4)

In Kapitel 4 lernt der Leser drei unterschiedliche Facetten der Figur Gatsby kennen: als Durchschnittsperson, als potenziellen Kriminellen und als romantischen Liebhaber und Träumer. Die drei Seiten werden in drei Szenen des vierten Kapitels deutlich (Fahrt mit Nick nach New York, Treffen mit Wolfshiem und Nicks Gespräch mit Jordan über Daisys und Gatsbys Vergangenheit). Da der Roman eine Reihe interessanter *clues* enthält, die Vorahnungen und Vermutungen über den weiteren Verlauf der Handlung anregen, bietet es sich an, diese im Unterricht für kreative Zwecke zu nutzen. Den roten Faden während der Lektüre des vierten Kapitels bildet ein Zitat Nicks aus dem ersten Kapitel, das den Schülerinnen und Schülern als Einstieg präsentiert wird und zu Spekulationen über die Person Gatsby einlädt. Es wird nach jedem Abschnitt des vierten Kapitels (s. o.) neu mit Ideen gefüllt.

In order to build suspense and make a story more interesting, writers often use techniques such as foreshadowing (or hints and clues of events to occur later in the plot). When authors give these hints and clues, we can make a prediction (or an educated guess) as to what will happen next.

The following example is taken from the first chapter of the novel, in which Nick first talks about Gatsby. Read the passage closely, sum up the quote in your own words and, finally, predict what you think will happen later in the story to Gatsby. Focus on the underlined clue and make notes on your ideas.

‚No – <u>Gatsby turned out all right in the end</u>; it is what <u>preyed on</u> Gatsby, what <u>foul dust</u> floated in the wake of <u>his dreams</u> that temporarily closed out my interest in the abortive sorrows and short-winded elations of men.'

Summary: In Nick's eyes, Gatsby turned out to be a decent person; what ended up bothering Nick were the cruel people (Who? What do they do?) and sad events (What happens to him?) that took place surrounding Gatsby making him sick and tired of the people around him.

Das vierte Kapitel (abzüglich des ersten Abschnitts, s. **Component 2**) wird nun in arbeitsteiliger Gruppenarbeit bearbeitet, um dann abschließend gemeinsam das Einstiegszitat auf der Grundlage der neuen Informationen zu kommentieren.

Gruppe 1: Read p. 47: 37 to p. 51: 32 closely.

1. What is this passage about? Decide on a one-sentence summary of this part.

2. What new information does Gatsby give Nick about himself? List at least 5 important pieces of information.

3. What is Nick's reaction to Gatsby's story?

Be prepared to present your findings to your classmates.

Gruppe 2: Read p. 51: 33 – p. 55: 9 closely.

1. What is this passage about? Decide on a one-sentence summary of this part.
2. Describe Mr Wolfshiem. Why do you think he is associated with Gatsby?

Be prepared to present your findings to your classmates.

Gruppe 3: Read p. 55: 10 – end of chapter 4.

1. What is this passage about? Decide on a one-sentence summary of this part.
2. Make a time line of the events that Jordan talks about to Nick (starting in October 1917 and concluding with the year 1922).
3. What did Gatsby want Jordan to ask Nick? What does Gatsby want Daisy to see?

Be prepared to present your findings to your classmates.

Lösungsvorschläge

Gruppe 1

1. This passage is about Nick and Gatsby driving to New York when Gatsby tells Nick his version of his lifestory.

2. He was brought up in America but educated at Oxford; son of a wealthy family in Midwest (all dead); suffered from a mysterious, very sad experience; attempted to forget it; travelled the world hunting, collecting jewels, and paintings; fought in WWI; claims to have won honours and medals.

3. Nick is sceptical and thinks Gatsby is lying

Gruppe 2

1. This part describes the lunch Nick and Gatsby are having with Meyer Wolfshiem in New York.

2. Meyer Wolfshiem is described as a small, flat nosed Jew with a large head, hairy nostrils, and tiny eyes. He supposedly fixed the 1919 World Series; he does business with Gatsby; they met after the War. The description is reminiscent of anti-semitic caricatures of that era.

Gruppe 3

1. The last part of chapter 4 is about Jordan Baker telling Nick about Daisy, her love affair with Gatsby in Louisville and her marriage to Tom Buchanan. She also reveals to Nick Gatsby's elaborate plan to see Daisy again.

2. Oct 1917: beginning of romantic love affair between Daisy Fay and Jay Gatsby; 1918: wild rumours that Daisy had wanted to go to New York to say good-bye to Gatsby, but had been prevented; Feb 1919: Daisy was engaged to Tom; June 1919: Daisy marries Tom B.; on the evening preceding the wedding she was found drunk and crying on her bed with a letter from Gatsby in her hand, wanting to call off the wedding; Aug 1919: back from her honeymoon, the Buchanans seemed to be happy; shortly afterwards Tom had an affair with a chambermaid; Apr 1920: their daughter was born, they all moved to France for a year; 1921: the Buchanans lived in Chicago, where Daisy was very popular; 1922: Daisy hears the name Gatsby again.

3. He wanted to ask Nick if he could arrange a meeting with Daisy and Gatsby at his house; Gatsby wants Daisy to see the enormity of his mansion and everything he has to offer.

Die Schülerinnen und Schüler informieren sich nun gegenseitig über ihre neuen Erkenntnisse hinsichtlich der Figur Gatsbys. Folgende Aspekte werden abschließend diskutiert:

1. Discuss the following questions in your group:
   - Why does Gatsby tell all these lies?
   - Why does he not simply invite Daisy to his house?
   - Why does he throw the parties?

2. Based on your reading, decide on a new prediction as to what Nick means when he talks about Gatsby in the opening paragraphs of the novel (quote, see above)! As a group, write what you predict will happen in one paragraph.

Lösungsvorschläge zu 1

- He probably tries to establish an upper-class identity for himself in order to impress Nick and disperse all rumours about him
- He is probably too shy to invite her in person.
- He tries to get her to come to one of his parties so they could be together again, wants to show off his wealth.

Abschließend äußern sich die Schülerinnen und Schüler vor dem Hintergrund ihrer Kenntnisse über die Romanfiguren zu folgendem Zitat Nicks:

'There are only the pursued, the pursuing, the busy and the tired.'

What is meant by this statement? In terms of the novel, who are the ones being pursued, the ones doing the pursuing, the ones who are busy, and the ones who are tired? Explain your interpretation in a few sentences.

Lösungsvorschlag:

People are usually either seeking something (such as love, wealth etc.) or being chased for something (love, wealth etc.). Both groups are busy and tired, miserable, sad etc.

Gatsby is pursuing love
Daisy is being pursued, tired of her life with Tom
Jordan is busy with her parties and sports
Myrtle is pursuing wealth and tired of her grey life with George
George is pursuing love, sad because of his disrespectful wife Myrtle
Nick is maybe tired of being in the middle of it all (?)

Read and respond

Have you ever experienced a time when you were pursuing something extremely important to you? What was it and what kind of obstacles did you have to face? What were your feelings like? Can you relate to any of the characters of *The Great Gatsby*?
Write about your experience in your reading journal.

In Vorbereitung auf den nächsten Unterrichtsschritt lesen die Schüler Kapitel 5 und bearbeiten *Copy 15*.

3.2 Playmaking: the reunion (chapter 5)

Das fünfte Kapitel stellt mit der Wiederbegegnung von Daisy und Gatsby den ersten Höhepunkt der Handlung dar. Da das Geschehen und das emotionale Auf und Ab von Daisy, aber besonders von Gatsby sehr exzessiv und transparent vom Erzähler beschrieben wird, bietet es sich förmlich an, das erste Treffen der beiden von den Schülerinnen und Schülern nachspielen zu lassen. Zur inhaltlichen Vorbereitung und Sicherung muss vorab die Hausaufgabe verglichen werden.

Lösungsvorschläge *Copy 15*

Model analysis	Reference to the novel
The Reunion	
Chapter five of The Great Gatsby is a central chapter in the novel as it describes the **decisive** moment when Gatsby sees Daisy again for the first time after five years. His dream, the image he has made himself of her, is confronted with reality. Although the meeting is to appear totally **casual**, Gatsby's preparations are very **thorough**: Nick's lawn is professionally cut and **abundant** flower bouquets are sent to his house. He gives his own house a **critical** inspection, too.	→ p. 61: 42 ('a greenhouse arrived from Gatsby's, …')
When the day has arrived, Gatsby is **nervous and overtired**. Twice he almost gives up and wants to run away. He does not feel up to facing the situation. Only Nick's **stern** admonitions prevent him from taking flight.	→ p. 62: 1 f. → p. 62: 24 ff.
Upon her arrival, Daisy is led to Gatsby's house by Nick. To Nick's (and the reader's) surprise, Gatsby has disappeared. Suddenly there is a knock on the front door and when Nick opens it he finds Gatsby, looking **pale**, shy, and even scared and **intimidated**. The scene has quite a comic and funny effect since the great Gatsby is behaving like a little boy. We would not expect such **helpless** behaviour from somebody who has made a fortune, who is determined, even **shrewd** in his business dealings.	→ p. 63: 14–22
The first stage of the meeting is **embarrassing** and strained on all sides. Gatsby is standing nervously against the mantelpiece; Daisy talks in an unnatural and anxious manner.	→ p. 63: 23–41
When Nick re-enters the house half an hour later the situation has totally changed. Daisy is **joyful**, Gatsby is glowing with happiness. The two lovers are completely absorbed with each other.	→ p. 65: 25 ff.
In the third stage of the meeting, the emotional tension of the two lovers explodes in two **hysterical** outbursts. When they all make a tour through Gatsby's mansion, he suddenly starts laughing, **relieved** after a period of such great tension and strain. When they enter his bedroom, Daisy starts crying over Gatsby's **elegant** shirts. She seems to be overwhelmed by his **faithful** endurance and unrelenting dedication.	→ p. 67: 4 ff. → p. 67: 29 ff.

63

Model analysis	Reference to the novel
At the end of the chapter Nick leaves the two lovers to themselves. This could be the happy ending of a sentimental novel; however, Gatsby seems to become **sceptical**: at the end, Nick observes that Gatsby is becoming aware of the discrepancy between dream and reality.	→ p. 69: 42 ff.

Im Mittelpunkt des folgenden Unterrichtsschrittes steht die szenische Umsetzung der Wiederbegegnung. Es bietet sich an, das Kapitel in einzelne Szenen zu unterteilen und auf verschiedene Schülergruppen aufzuteilen (z. B. Gespräch Nick-Gatsby vor Daisys Auftritt, erste Phase der Wiederbegegnung; Daisy & Gatsby nach der Rückkehr Nicks; Rundgang durch das Haus etc.).

Um den Schülerinnen und Schülern zu verdeutlichen, dass sie für das szenische Spielen den Romantext nicht nur in Dialogform umwandeln müssen, sondern vor allem Bühnenanweisungen erarbeiten müssen, erhalten sie zur Einstimmung folgenden Arbeitsauftrag:

Die Schülerinnen und Schüler erhalten Wortkarten mit verschiedenen Adjektiven zur Beschreibung von Gefühlen sowie eine Auswahl an Textstreifen (siehe *Copy 16, part I*). Jeder Schüler zieht nun eine Karte mit einem Adjektiv und einen Textstreifen. Ihre Aufgabe ist es nun, den Textauszug in der jeweiligen Stimmung zu präsentieren. Die anderen Schüler müssen erraten, in welcher Stimmung der Satz gesprochen wurde. Erweitert werden kann die Übung durch Bewegungsanweisungen, die ebenfalls Gefühle ausdrücken.

Nun erarbeiten die Schüler mithilfe von *Copy 16 (part II)* einen eigenen Drehbuchausschnitt auf der Basis der Romanvorlage.

Im Anschluss präsentieren die Gruppen ihre Stücke, die dann von den Zuschauern mit der Romanvorlage verglichen werden können.

Alternativ können die Drehbücher auch kopiert und unter den Schülergruppen getauscht werden. Als Hausaufgabe bereiten sich die Schüler dann auf die Präsentation der neuen Szene vor. In der Folgestunde spielen die Gruppen dann ihre Interpretionen des Drehbuches der Gruppe vor, die sie ursprünglich verfasst hat. Im Anschluss erhalten die ‚Schauspieler‘ und ‚Drehbuchautoren‘ ausreichend Zeit, um über die Interpretation zu diskutieren.

Read and respond

"Possibly it had occurred to him that the colossal significance of that light had vanished forever … Now it was again a green light on a dock." (68: 8 ff.)

1. Describe how Gatsby's life seems to have changed after his reunion with Daisy.

2. Write down two more quotes from chapter 5 that illustrate this change.

3. In your opinion, is winning Daisy a triumph or a tragedy for Gatsby?

4. How can you relate to these quotes?

3.3 Analysing symbols

Der Roman enthält eine Fülle an tiefgründigen Symbolen, die ihn wie einen roten Faden durchlaufen. Nach der Lektüre des fünften Kapitels sind den Schülerinnen und Schüler mittlerweile eine Reihe wichtiger Symbole begegnet, sodass diese nun auf der Basis der Lektüre thematisiert werden können.

Falls der Begriff des Symbols bislang nicht definiert wurde, erfolgt der Einstieg recht anschaulich mittels eines konkreten Objekts, z. B. einer Rose, die bekanntlich für die abstrakte Idee der ‚Liebe' steht.

Try to explain in your own words what is meant when we say 'the rose is a symbol of love'.

A symbol is something concrete (a person or an object) that is used to represent an abstract idea. For example, a red rose is a conventional symbol of love. Its pleasant smell may represent the sweetness, delicateness of love; its thorns, however, may symbolize the hurt and sufferings that can result from an unhappy love.

Nun erfolgt die Überleitung zum Roman, dessen Symbole im nächsten Schritt in einer *placemat activity* auf der Basis des bislang Gelesenen erläutert werden.

Die Schülerinnen und Schüler werden dafür in Viergruppen eingeteilt, die jeweils mindestens ein Symbol erarbeiten. Auf der vorbereiteten *placemat* für jede Gruppe steht in der Mitte ein Symbol:

- the green light
- Gatsby's house
- Gatsby's library of uncut books
- the eyes of Dr Eckleburg
- Gatsby's shirts
- the Valley of Ashes
- West Egg
- East Egg

Die Schülerinnen und Schüler erhalten nun eine Liste möglicher symbolischer Bedeutungen *(Copy 17)*. Sie haben nun die Aufgabe, individuell dem zentralen Symbol eine ihrer Meinung nach schlüssige Bedeutung zuzuordnen und auf der Basis der Lektüre zu begründen. Da die Zuordnung nicht immer eindeutig ist, ist zu erwarten, dass die Gruppenmitglieder zu unterschiedlichen Ergebnissen kommen und sich dann in der zweiten Phase auf eine Bedeutung einigen müssen. Die Kopiervorlag*e Copy 17* präsentiert Ideen für die Vorbereitung der einzelnen *placemats* sowie die Arbeitsaufträge für die Schülerinnen und Schüler.

Lösungsvorschläge *Copy 17*

the green light:
- 'old' money: light is located at the end of Daisy's dock in East Egg
- hope/aspirations: the hope that Gatsby will be reunited with Daisy in the end; visual substitute for Daisy, who he cannot see.

Gatsby's house:
- 'new' money: located in West Egg
- wealth: Gatsby's house is over the top in design.

Gatsby's library of uncut books:
- false pretences: Gatsby has not cut the books and left them on the shelves for display purposes; this shows that Gatsby wants people to believe that he is well-educated, but upon closer look, the books are unread.

The eyes of Dr Eckleburg:
- God: they watch over everything that is happening in the Valley of Ashes. Because it is an inanimate object, it cannot make judgments but hovers over as a reminder that the characters' actions are being watched.
- poverty: the sign is located in the Valley of Ashes and is run-down after the doctor who placed the ad went out of business or moved away.

Gatsby's shirts:
- success: they show how far Gatsby has come that he can spend money so extravagantly now.
- crime/corruption: he has obtained his wealth to buy the shirts by less-than-lawful means.
- wealth: Gatsby had these shirts made of fine materials and monogrammed.
- hope/aspirations: Gatsby shows Daisy his shirts to impress her, hoping she will see all she has missed by not being with him.
- materialism: Gatsby chooses to show her the shirts so she can see what he has bought with his money; he is trying to show off to impress her because he knows she is impressed by material objects.

The Valley of Ashes:
- death: it is described as a dark, desolate place; ashes can symbolize death.
- moral decay: the place where Tom meets up with Myrtle for their affair.
- poverty: the poor, working-class Wilsons live there.

West Egg:
- represents 'new money'; area where Nick and Gatsby are living; symbolizes newly aquired wealth.

East Egg:
- area where the Buchanans are residing; symbolizes 'old money' and wealth that has been inherited for many generations.

Read and respond

For Jay Gatsby, the green light at the end of the dock symbolizes the upper-class woman he longs for. What is *your* green light? What do you strive for – to want to be someone you're not, to want to achieve something that's just beyond reach, whether it's professional success or wealth or idealized love or …? Write about your green light in your reading journal.

 Als Vorbereitung auf die folgende Stunde lesen die Schülerinnen und Schüler Kapitel 6 und bearbeiten *Copy 18*.

3.4 Understanding Gatsby's youth (chapter 6)

Bevor die Schüler die wahre Herkunft Gatsbys, die im ersten Teil des Kapitels 6 von Nick geschildert wird, erarbeiten, erfolgt die Sicherung der Hausaufgabe.

Lösungsvorschläge *Copy 18*

part (part 1: to be left out)
part 2: pp. 73: 32 – 75: 34;   title: Visitors on horseback
part 3: pp. 75: 35 – 79: 12;   title: The second Gatsby party
part 4: pp: 79: 13 – end;   title: The beginning of the love affair

1. After many weeks of not seeing Gatsby	Nick goes to visit him.
2. Shortly after his arrival, Tom Buchanan and two others on a horseback ride	show up for a drink.

3. They exchange some social small talk	wherein Gatsby is invited to dine with the group.
4. The three riders abruptly leave without Gatsby	because they are taken aback that he accepted what they deem to be a purely rhetorical question.
5. Because he is apparently concerned with his wife's recent activities,	Tom accompanies Daisy to one of Gatsby's parties.
6. Gatsby tries to impress the Buchanans by	pointing out all the celebrities present.
7. Then he makes a point of introducing Tom	much to his unease, as the 'polo player.'
8. First Gatsby and Daisy dance,	later, they adjourn to Nick's stairs for a half-hour of privacy.
9. When they head back to the party	Tom remarks he wishes to have dinner with another group.
10. Daisy, who is always aware of what Tom is really up to,	offers a pencil in case he wants to take down an address.
11. Daisy, aside from the half-hour she spent with Gatsby, finds the party	unnerving and appalling.
12. After the Buchanans leave and the party breaks up, Nick and Gatsby	review the evening.
13. Gatsby worries about Daisy and their future	because he fears that she did not have a good time.
14. The chapter concludes with a second flashback that describes the	beginning of Gatsby's and Daisy's romantic love.

Die Untersuchung von Gatsbys Vergangenheit erfolgt in zwei Schritten: Zunächst erhalten die Schüler verschiedene Bilder, die alle etwas mit der Jugend Gatsbys zusammenhängen. Auf der Basis dieser visuellen Hilfen verfassen die Schülerinnen und Schüler in der *while-reading*-Phase eine Zusammenfassung der Jugendzeit Gatsbys. Die Arbeitsaufträge und Bilder sind auf *Copy 19* zusammengestellt. Nach einer Präsentation der Ergebnisse lesen die Schülerinnen und Schüler den ersten Teil des Kapitels und vergleichen sie mit ihrer Version.

Lösungsvorschläge *Copy 19*

Gatsby, whose real name is James Gatz, comes from North Dakota; son of poor farmers; from the age of 16, young James tries his luck as a clam-digger and a salmon-fisher; early on he has affairs with women; when he is 17 years old he meets 50-year-old Dan Cody on the shores of Lake Superior; he takes Gatsby under his wing and prepares him for the yachting life; they embark for the West Indies and Barbary Coast; they spend five years together; they go around the continent three times; Cody dies in a mysterious way; Gatsby inherits $ 25,000 after Cody's death but due to some legal problems he never receives the money; however, Cody remains his 'mentor' who will have crucial impact on his future life.

Vertiefend werden nun die Aspekte der Vergangenheit Gatsbys besprochen:

1. What role does Dan Cody play in Gatsby's life and his dreams?

Dan Cody is the typical self-made man of the West who accumulated a vast fortune through hard work and brutal methods. He becomes Gatsby's mentor, 'best friend' and ultimately his 'destiny.'

2. To what degree does the story we are told now differ from what we already know?

He did not go to Oxford, does not come from a wealthy family, is not orphaned, ...

Abschließend ist es für das Verständnis der Hauptfigur und den weiteren Verlauf des Romans dringend erforderlich, Gatsbys Traum und den darauf basierenden Identitätswandel zu analysieren. Das folgende Zitat sowie eine Zusatzinformation zu Plato sollen den Schülerinnen und Schülern helfen, Gatsbys Zustand besser zu verstehen. Folgendes wird auf einer Folie präsentiert:

"The truth was that Jay Gatsby of West Egg, Long Island, sprang from his Platonic conception of himself. He was a son of God – a phrase which, if it means anything, means just that – and he must be about His Father's business, the service of a vast, vulgar, meretricious beauty. So he invented just the sort of Jay Gatsby that a seventeen year-old boy would be likely to invent, and to this conception he was faithful to the end." (p. 71: 34–41)

Plato held the view that REALITY was an imperfect reflection of an ideal, permanent realm. According to him, only IDEAS were really real. With this in mind, what would you say Nick means when he says, "Jay Gatsby sprang from his Platonic conception of himself?"

Gatsby renounces his former life and origin and creates (almost godlike) a new identity for himself, symbolized by his new name. Just like Plato, Gatsby believes that reality can be formed solely by the imagination. Therefore, Gatsby believes that his 'ideal self' is his real, perfect self.

Zur vertiefenden Anwendung (evtl. Hausaufgabe) analysieren die Schülerinnen und Schüler eine weitere Textpassage des 6. Kapitels:

"But his heart … that the rock of the world was founded securely on a fairy's wing." (p. 72: 10–20)

Gatsby believes in the 'unreality of reality', that the 'rock of the world' (= the material world) is founded on a 'fairy's wing (= a dream world, a world of imagination). Again, Gatsby's Platonic conception of the world and of himself are emphasized. According to his romantic belief, 'mind' is given priority over 'matter'; or: ideals, visions, dreams, are what really matter.

Abschließend nehmen die Schülerinnen und Schüler persönlich Stellung zu Gatsbys Auffassung von Vergangenheit.

Read and respond

"You can't repeat the past." –
"Can't repeat the past?" Gatsby cried incredulously. "Why of course you can!"
Do you agree with Nick or Gatsby?
Have you ever experienced a time when you wanted to relive or change a moment from your past? Write about that experience in your reading journal.

While-reading task: chapter 5

1. **Read chapter 5 of** *The Great Gatsby* **closely.**

2. **Study the model analysis of chapter 5 given below thoroughly: it is a thorough summary and analysis of chapter 5. However, nearly each adjective has been deleted. Complete the text by filling in the missing expressions from the box.**

3. **Not only were adjectives removed but important quotes that support the various statements are also missing. Take a red pen and include the corresponding pages and lines by writing them into the right-hand margin.**

> sceptical ■ faithful ■ intimidated ■ helpless ■ shrewd ■ embarrassing and strained
> ■ joyful ■ thorough ■ absorbed ■ decisive ■ pale ■ stern ■ casual ■ abundant ■ critical
> ■ nervous and overtired ■ hysterical ■ elegant ■ relieved

The Reunion

Chapter five of *The Great Gatsby* is a central chapter in the novel as it describes the _____ moment when Gatsby sees Daisy again for the first time after five years. His dream, the image he has made himself of her, is confronted with reality.

Although the meeting is to appear totally _____ Gatsby's preparations are very _____: Nick's lawn is professionally cut and _____ flower bouquets are sent to his house. He gives his own house a _____ inspection too.

When the day has arrived, Gatsby is _____ . Twice he almost gives up and wants to run away. He does not feel up to facing the situation. Only Nick's _____ admonitions prevent him from taking flight.

Upon her arrival, Daisy is led to Gatsby's house by Nick. To Nick's (and the reader's) surprise, Gatsby has disappeared. Suddenly there is a knock on the front door and when Nick opens it he finds Gatsby, looking _____, shy, and even scared and _____ The scene has quite a comic and funny effect since the great Gatsby is behaving like a little boy. We would not expect such _____ behaviour from somebody who has made a fortune, who is determined, even _____ in his business dealings.

The first stage of the meeting is _____ on all sides. Gatsby is is standing nervously against the mantelpiece Daisy talks in an unnatural and anxious manner.

When Nick re-enters the house half an hour later the situation has totally changed. Daisy is _____, Gatsby is glowing with happiness. The two lovers are completely _____ with each other.

In the third stage of the meeting, the emotional tension of the two lovers explodes in two _____ outbursts. When they all make a tour through Gatsby's mansion, he suddenly starts laughing, _____ after a period of such great tension and strain. When they enter his bedroom, Daisy starts crying over Gatsby's _____ shirts. She seems to be overwhelmed by his _____ endurance and unrelenting dedication.

At the end of the chapter Nick leaves the two lovers to themselves. This could be the happy ending of a sentimental novel; however, Gatsby seems to become _____: at the end, Nick observes that Gatsby is becoming aware of the discrepancy between dream and reality.

Playmaking part I: Read it out!

Example for adjectives/movements:

- surprised
- fearful, moving back
- relieved, moving forward
- devastated
- angry
- overjoyed
- relaxed
- shy
- upset
- dreamily, staring out of the window

- excited, glowing
- nervous, moving around restlessly
- bored, rolling eyes
- embarrassed, biting finger nails
- shocked, shaking
- surprised
- worried, sweating
- tense
- confused
- ...

Sample sentences to be read out:

- "Oh! It's you!"
- "See what you've done!"
- "Why don't you just leave her alone?"
- "I'm not gonna give it up."

Playmaking part II: Act it out!

In groups you are asked to transform one (or more) scene(s) of Gatsby's and Daisy's reunion into a play script with clear instructions to the actors on how to play their parts. The script must be written out clearly. To do this you will have to …

- remove any descriptive parts from the novel text,
- add instructions on how the character should speak the lines,
- give instructions on where the people are sitting, standing, and how they move.
- Your interpretation of the given scene must be plausible within the frame of the novel.

One example has been done for you (based on p. 61: 42 – p. 62: 5):

(Nick is relaxing in his living room when suddenly Gatsby appears at the front door. He hurries in with a scared look on his face. Before he starts speaking he looks nervously around the room.)

GATSBY: *(speaking fast)* Is everything all right?

NICK: *(putting aside his newspaper, looking up to Gatsby)* The grass looks fine, if that's what you mean.

GATSBY: *(dreamily, looking out of the window)* What grass? Oh, the grass in the yard.
...

Decide who of you is going to perform which role and practise your lines well.

Symbolism

1. Match the symbol written down in the centre of the paper with its symbolic meaning. Write down your idea on your section of the placemat and explain your choice. Support your ideas by giving evidence from the novel. There may be more than one correct answer for the symbol.

2. When everybody in your group is finished, start reading the others' ideas by turning the paper clockwise so that you have always got a new section in front of you.

3. Then discuss your ideas and try to agree on a result which you write into the free space in the centre of the placemat. Select someone from your group to present your results.

Useful phrases for talking about symbolism:
- a symbol represents sth./stands for sth.
- sth. serves as a symbol of/for …
- the symbolic meaning of sth is …
- sth. is presented symbolically

Symbolic meanings:
- 'old' money
- hope/aspirations
- power
- materialism
- death
- success
- honesty
- crime/corruption
- moral decay
- wealth
- God
- poverty
- 'new' money
- false pretences

While-reading task: chapter 6

1. Read chapter 6 but leave out the first section (start on p. 73: 32).

2. The chapter consists of four separated parts. Locate these parts by writing down the corresponding lines and find a title for each part (except for the first one).

   (Part 1: to be left out)

   part 2:   p.   –

   title: _____

   part 3:   p.   –

   title: _____

   part 4:   p.   –

   title: _____

3. **Based on your reading, connect the correct sentence halves.**

1. After many weeks of not seeing Gatsby …	beginning of Gatsby's and Daisy's romantic love.
2. Shortly after his arrival, Tom Buchanan and two others on a horseback ride …	because they are taken aback that he accepted what they deem to be a purely rhetorical question.
3. They exchange some social small talk …	unnerving and appalling.
4. The three riders abruptly leave without Gatsby …	show up for a drink.
5. Because he is apparently concerned with his wife's recent activities, …	much to his unease, as the 'polo player.'
6. Gatsby tries to impress the Buchanans by …	Tom accompanies Daisy to one of Gatsby's parties.
7. Then he makes a point of introducing Tom …	offers a pencil in case he wants to take down an address.
8. First Gatsby and Daisy dance, …	later, they adjourn to Nick's stairs for a half-hour of privacy.
9. When they head back to the party …	Tom remarks he wishes to have dinner with another group.
10. Daisy, who is always aware of what Tom is really up to, …	pointing out all the celebrities present.
11. Daisy, aside from the half-hour she spent with Gatsby, finds the party …	Nick goes to visit him.
12. After the Buchanans leave and the party breaks up, Nick and Gatsby …	wherein Gatsby is invited to dine with the group.
13. Gatsby worries about Daisy and their future …	review the evening.
14. The chapter concludes with a second flashback that describes the …	because he fears that she did not have a good time.

The story of Gatsby's youth

So far, Jay Gatsby seems to be a very mysterious character: We do not really know anything specific about him, just rumours that are spread on different occasions. There is, however, a real truth about his youth and family background that the narrator is about to share with the reader.

1. The following pictures and symbols tell the story of Gatsby's youth. Write a summary of Gatsby's early biography based on your interpretation of the given hints. Remember to use the present tense and make use of suitable connectives to link your ideas.

2. Share your ideas with the rest of the class and discuss similarities and differences.

3. Now turn to the opening paragraphs of chapter 6 and compare Nick's report to your biography. Which pictures did you guess correctly? Which aspects surprised you?

North Dakota

17 years old

to dig

to surround the continent

R.I.P.

25,000 dollars

Gatsby's fight for his dream

4.1 Tom vs. Gatsby: structure of the plot (chapter 7)

Kapitel 7 stellt zum einen den Höhe- und Wendepunkt der Haupthandlung insgesamt dar; zum anderen ist das Kapitel in sich eine Abfolge von schnell aufeinander folgenden Episoden, die zusammen betrachtet mit einer klassischen Dramenstruktur verglichen werden können. Vor diesem Hintergrund (und auch, weil es das längste Kapitel des Romans bildet) wird Kapitel 7 in zwei Schritten untersucht: Zunächst erfolgt eine Analyse der Gesamtstruktur des Kapitels, dann die genaue Betrachtung einzelner Aspekte. Inhaltlich steht dabei die Frage im Mittelpunkt, warum Gatsby den Kampf um Daisy gegen Tom verliert.

Die Schülerinnen und Schüler lesen (evtl. als vorbereitende Hausaufgabe) Kapitel 7 und erhalten dann im Unterricht *Copy 20*. In Partnerarbeit überprüfen sie ihr Textverständnis anhand der Stichpunkte.

> **Lösungsvorschläge** *Copy 20*
>
> 1–4:
>
> - "the whole caravansary had fallen in like a card house" (p. 81: 31):
>   Nick about the ending of Gatsby's summer parties; reason: Daisy disapproves of the parties
> - lunch at the Buchanans' house:
>   Nick is invited to have lunch at the Buchanans' house with Gatsby
> - "You look so cool … You always look so cool." (p. 85: 5–9):
>   Daisy to Gatsby, inside her house
> - "His hand, trembling with his effort at self-control, bore to his lips the last of his glass of ale." (p. 85: 22f.):
>   Tom when he realizes that Gatsby has an affair with his wife; foreshadowing of the confrontation
> - "circus wagon" (p. 86: 30):
>   They decide to go to NYC. As they depart, they switch cars: Nick, Jordan and Tom take Gatsby's 'circus wagon'
> - "small investigation on this fellow" (p. 87: 3):
>   On their way to NYC, Tom has become suspicious of Gatsby and has had him investigated.
> - "I'm going to get her away." (p. 88: 14f.):
>   Tom stops at Wilson's garage. George abruptly announces he and Myrtle will be heading West shortly because he has just learned of her secret life.
> - "her eyes, wide with jealous terror" (p. 89: 7):
>   Myrtle is locked into her room; mistakes Jordan for Daisy when she looks at Tom, Jordan, Nick stopping for gas at the garage
> - Plaza Hotel
>   The group assembles in the Plaza Hotel in New York.
> - "Your wife doesn't love you. […] She's never loved you. She loves me." (p. 93: 8f.):

After Tom has confronted Gatsby about his love for Daisy, Gatsby refuses to be intimidated and fights back.

- "You're revolting." (p. 94: 1):
  Daisy to Tom; tries to hold on to Gatsby
- "Oh, you want too much!" (p. 94: 28):
  Daisy to Gatsby; Daisy is turning away from Gatsby
- "The God damned coward! [...] He didn't even stop his car." (p. 100: 44 f.):
  Tom, sobbing, when he realizes it was Gatsby's car which had hit Myrtle and caused her death.
- "natural intimacy" (p. 103: 21):
  Later, at the Buchanans' house, Tom and Daisy are sitting in the kitchen, impression of peace and calm
- "sacred vigil over nothing" (p. 103: 35):
  Gatsby is unconcerned about Myrtle's death but only worried about Daisy and her well-being, but, without hope

5.

Chapter 7 consists of five distinct episodes similar to the five-act structure of the classical drama:

- Act I (exposition)   lunch at the Buchanans':
  conflict becomes apparent when Tom realizes that Daisy had told Gatsby that she loves him
- Act II (rising action)   ride to New York:
  prepares the ground for the catastrophe in Act IV: Wilson wants to take his wife to the West and Myrtle is led to believe that Gatsby's car is Tom's. This causes her to run in front of Gatsby's car in order to speak with Tom.
- Act III (turning point)   dispute between Tom and Gatsby
- Act IV (falling action/
  catastrophe)   Myrtle's death
- Act V   Gatsby's defeat

Auf der Grundlage der Kenntnisse kann nun abschließend die Entscheidung Daisys gegen Gatsby thematisiert werden. Da der Roman mit der Konfrontation im Plaza Hotel (noch) nicht zu Ende ist und die Entscheidung mehrere Gründe haben könnte, bietet es sich an, dass jeder Schüler individuell eine Begründung notiert, um diese dann im weiteren Verlauf der Lektüre zu überprüfen, zu erweitern, zu bestätigen etc. Die Ideen können wahlweise eingesammelt werden, um ein Meinungsbild zu erstellen, das zu einem späteren Zeitpunkt erneut evaluiert wird (z. B. am Ende der Lektüre).
Die Schülerinnen und Schüler erhalten folgenden Arbeitsauftrag:

Why does Daisy stay with Tom? Why did she change her mind?
Reread the scene at the Plaza Hotel and make notes on Tom's and Gatsby's charges and strategies against each other.
Include your knowledge on Daisy's character in your consideration.
Write one paragraph that sums up your opinion and hand it in to your teacher.
You need not write down your name.

Lösungsvorschläge

- Gatsby asks too much of her (he forces Daisy to disclaim her own past with Tom and therefore a part of her own identity).

- Gatsby has a connection to the underworld, is a liar (as Tom shows during their argument: Gatsby is not an Oxford man, rootless parvenu, involved in criminal activities).
- her fear of losing her social status

Verschiedene *post-reading activities* bieten sich je nach Schwerpunktsetzung an:

1. Surprisingly, Tom does not interfere when Gatsby follows Daisy and they both return home together in Gatsby's yellow car. Think of ways for Gatsby to win Daisy in the end.

   He might try to convince her of Tom's negative character traits or recall their happy past; he could stress his accomplishments and luxurious way of living to appeal to her.

2. Anticipate Gatsby's future: when he returns home, he writes a letter to Nick in which he shares his feelings and plans for the future. Write this letter.

   He feels devastated, depressed, broken
   = moves away, sells his possessions, commits suicide, attacks Tom.

Schüler können auf der Grundlage verschiedener Anspielungen aber auch zu dem Schluss kommen, dass Gatsby die Entscheidung von Daisy nicht realisiert und akzeptiert, weil er damit seine Identität, die ja auf seinem Traum aufbaut, verlieren würde.

3. Contrast the situation inside and outside the Buchanans' house at the end of chapter 7: what is revealed about the characters? Give evidence from the text to support your analysis.

   Inside:
   Tom and Daisy sit together in the kitchen, united by an "unmistakable air of natural intimacy"; "his hand had fallen upon and covered her own";
   = impression of peaceful idyll, of a sheltered existence; Tom has re-established their old relationship.
   The scene confirms that Gatsby has lost Daisy forever; peacefulness may be interpreted as a sign that both are completely blind to any kind of social responsibilty (considering what has happened to both of them just before).

   Outside:
   Gatsby is "watching over nothing" for Daisy is neither endangered nor is she interested in him any more = pathetic, slightly comic, lonely and tragic figure. Gatsby is totally absorbed with Daisy, "He spoke as if Daisy's reaction was the only thing that mattered"; he is also totally unconcerned about Myrtle's death as the Buchanans.

Um den Kontrast der Atmosphären und Gefühlswelten zwischen den Figuren zu veranschaulichen, kann die Aufgabenstellung auch in zwei *freeze frames* umgesetzt werden. Wichtig ist dabei, dass ein weiterer Schüler als *ghost speaker* eingesetzt wird, der das ausspricht, was die Figuren des Standbilds in ihrem Inneren empfinden.

4.2 Writing a news story: the accident causing Myrtle's death

Da Wilson in der Handlung der folgenden Kapitel eine wichtige Rolle spielt (Myrtles Tod führt zu Gatsbys Tod, was der Leser aber noch nicht ahnt), sollten seine Situation und die Hintergründe des Todes seiner Frau näher beleuchtet werden. Es bietet sich an dieser Stelle an, die Schüler auf der Grundlage des Romans einen Zeitungsbericht verfassen zu lassen. Je nach Schwerpunktsetzung kann im Vorfeld ein Exkurs zu den unterschiedlichen Merkmalen von *popular* und *quality papers* stattfinden, die die Schüler dann in ihren Produkten realisieren. Das Verfassen von *news stories* eignet sich auch für die kreativ-produktive Auseinandersetzung mit Gatsbys und Wilsons Tod in Kapitel 8 und 9.

Um sich besser in die verzweifelte Lage Myrtles und auch ihres Ehemannes hineinversetzen zu können, erhalten die Schülerinnen und Schüler eingangs folgenden Arbeitsauftrag, den sie schriftlich individuell bearbeiten:

When Tom stops for gas at Wilson's garage, Myrtle sees him from the room in which she has been locked up by her husband. Write a 'cry-for-help'-note for Myrtle in which she tells Tom how she feels, why she is locked up and what she wants him to do.

Her note should include that her husband has found out about her affair and wants to move to another place to start a new life; she is terrified of the idea, though, because she is fed up with her marriage, detests her husband and her life, does not see any chance of changing her feelings etc.

Im Anschluss lesen die Schülerinnen und Schüler die Aussagen des Nachbarn Michaelis und verfassen auf dieser Basis eine *news story*. Die Lektüre und der Zeitungsbericht können auch auf die Reaktion von Wilson und Tom ausgeweitet werden (S. 98: 10 – S. 100: 45).

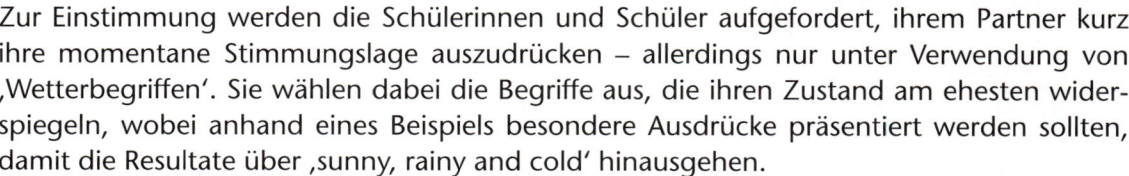

Examine the evidence surrounding the death of Mrytle Wilson by rereading p. 97: 1 to p. 98: 9. Write a newspaper article as it might appear in a quality or popular paper. Use the journalistic style your newspaper demands (intention, addressee, register, style, content, headline etc.)

4.3 Writing an analysis: symbolism

Wie in Kapitel 5 wird auch im 7. Kapitel die Wetterlage sehr ausführlich und präzise beschrieben. Da kein kausaler Zusammenhang zwischen Wetter und Handlung existiert, haben die Hinweise eine symbolische Bedeutung, schaffen eine bestimmte Atmosphäre und unterstützen die Handlung – was im folgenden Unterrichtsschritt analysiert wird.

Zur Einstimmung werden die Schülerinnen und Schüler aufgefordert, ihrem Partner kurz ihre momentane Stimmungslage auszudrücken – allerdings nur unter Verwendung von ‚Wetterbegriffen'. Sie wählen dabei die Begriffe aus, die ihren Zustand am ehesten widerspiegeln, wobei anhand eines Beispiels besondere Ausdrücke präsentiert werden sollten, damit die Resultate über ‚sunny, rainy and cold' hinausgehen.

Mögliche Ideen für die Formulierung eines ‚interior weather forecast': cloudy, unsettled, heavy rain, high wind, drizzle, dull/bright, foggy, a strong breeze, scattered showers, stormy, thunder, lightning, flooded, cleared up, sunny spells, freezing …

Daran anschließend untersuchen die Schülerinnen und Schüler die erste Szene des Kapitels *7 (lunch at the Buchanans)* hinsichtlich der Verwendung von Wetterbegriffen:

It is often said that 'rain and sunshine in novels are never accidental'. Does this apply to chapter 7 of *The Great Gatsby* as well?

Find quotes in the first part of the chapter that describe the weather (including temperature) on this day. Based on your analysis of the plot, how does the weather contribute to the general atmosphere?

Lösungsvorschläge

cool	hot
"The room was dark and cool." (p. 82: 36)	"The next day broiling." (p. 82: 3)
	"the simmering hush of noon" (p. 82:6)
"They certainly look cool." (p. 84: 15) "Ah," she cried, "you look so cool." (p. 85: 5f.)	"on the edge of combustion" (p. 82: 7)
	"Hot! … Hot! … Hot" (p. 82: 18)
"Tom came back, preceding four gin rickeys that clicked full of ice" (p. 84: 12)	"But it's so hot … everything's so confused …" (p. 84: 42)
= associated with the world of the Buchanans (though the heat cannot be kept outside completely) and with Gatsby and his vision	= The day of the conflict is symbolically characterized by oppressive heat. Later on, Daisy and Nick associate the heat with confusion; also suggestive of violence, aggressiveness.

Um die Schülerinnen und Schüler darauf vorzubereiten, eine eigene schriftliche Analyse der Sprache zu verfassen, erhalten sie eine Modellanalyse zu Kapitel 5, anhand derer sie passende Redewendungen, Aufbau und Struktur einer Analyse ableiten können *(Copy 21)*.

Lösungsvorschläge *Copy 21*

Structure: Each paragraph consists of three elements: POINT out a symbol, give EVIDENCE from the text (a quotation) and EXPLAIN the symbolic meaning or how it contributes to a certain effect that the author wants to achieve.

Language: to consist of …, to underline a certain atmosphere/effect/impression, to reflect sth., to symbolize sth./to become a symbol of sth., to emphasize/to stress sth., …

Auf der Basis dieser Übung verfassen sie nun eine eigene schriftliche Analyse der oben genannten Szene aus Kapitel 7.

4.4 Colours as symbols

Ein wesentliches Symbol, das den Roman auszeichnet, ist das Symbol der Farbe. Davon ausgehend, dass bestimmte Farben auch ganz bestimmte Assoziationen bei den Schülerinnen und Schülern hervorrufen, können diese Ideen zunächst gesammelt und dann mit dem Roman verglichen werden: Wie setzt der Autor Farben ein? Welche Assoziationen werden geweckt? Stimmen diese mit den Assoziationen der Schüler überein?

In einer *placemat activity* sammeln die Schülerinnen und Schüler in arbeitsteiliger Gruppenarbeit vorab ihre Assoziationen zu den Farben, die im Roman eine zentrale Rolle spielen (weiß, grün, golden, grau):

Individual work:
When you think of the colour white, what images come to your mind? List 5.
What abstract nouns or adjectives come to your mind? List 5.

Group work:
Read your group members' ideas and agree on 3 aspects for each task. Write
them down into the centre of the poster.

Lösungsvorschläge

white:	white dove, snow, wedding dress, whipped cream, paper, …
	clean, sterile, pure, innocent, peace, boring, calm, …
green:	grass, leaves, frog, green light, meadow,
	spring, freshness, life, safety, …
grey:	storm clouds, grey hair, dolphin, cement, stone, …
	seriousness, darkness, cloudy, ominous, depressed, …
gold/yellow:	sunlight, gold coins, jewelry, lemon, …
	wealth, happiness, warmth, comfort, …

Nun erfolgt in einem zweiten Schritt die Verknüpfung mit dem Roman. Dazu bleiben die
Gruppen bestehen, die sich auch weiterhin mit ‚ihrer' Farbe beschäftigen. Die Schülerinnen
und Schüler erhalten *Copy 22*, auf der verschiedene Textpassagen vorgestellt werden, die
mit dem Symbol der Farbe spielen. Die Gruppen erarbeiten die Auszüge und überprüfen,
inwiefern ihre eigenen Assoziationen widergespiegelt werden. In einer zweiten Phase werden nun neue Gruppen gebildet, in denen jeweils ‚eine Farbe' vertreten ist. Analog zur
Einstiegsphase befragen die Experten ihre Mitschülerinnen und Mitschüler nach ihren eigenen Assoziationen und präsentieren dann ihre Textpassagen und Interpretationen.

Lösungsvorschläge *Copy 22*

white:
The Buchanans' house is described as a "cheerful red-and-white Georgian Colonial mansion overlooking the bay." (p. 10: 43 ff.)
In chapter 1 Jordan describes when she met Daisy, "from Louisville. Our white
girlhood was together there. Our beautiful white –" (p. 19: 27 f.)
In chapter 4, Jordan reminisces about Daisy, "she dressed in white, and had a
little white roadster and all day long the telephone rang in her house and excited young officers from …" (p. 55: 24 ff.)
= Daisy is usually associated with the colour white (problematic because she is
not 'pure' or 'innocent' since she was the one who killed Myrtle and did not
confess her guilt), …

yellow/gold:
Gatsby's car is described as cream-coloured, then yellow.
Mrs Wilson's new dress is described as cream-coloured when she enters the
party
= initial ideas may not fit here because the objects are not purely/really 'wealthy',
do not display true happiness, …

grey:
Wilson's appearance as well as the Valley of Ashes are associated with the colour
grey
= ideas are reflected in the place/character, …

green:
the green light at the end of Daisy's dock
Michaelis told the first policeman that he believed the car that hit Myrtle was a light green.
Daisy jokes with Nick when she is at Gatsby's party.
= idea of hope is reflected well in the green light, …

Auf der Grundlage der neuen Erkenntnisse erarbeiten die Schülerinnen und Schüler dann individuell eine Antwort auf die Fragestellung:

Fitzgerald uses colour as a symbol throughout the whole novel. How is colour used to define the characters? How is it used to create the setting? How is it used to create mood? Explore Fitzgerald's use of colours as symbols and present at least one example for each aspect.

Natürlich kann die Erarbeitung auch in arbeitsgleicher Gruppen- oder Partnerarbeit erfolgen (sodass alle Schülerinnen und Schüler alle Textstellen erarbeiten).

4.5 Evaluating Gatsby's character (chapter 8)

Kapitel 8 besteht im Wesentlichen aus zwei Teilen: zum einen aus dem Rückblick auf Gatsbys vergangene Beziehung zu Daisy und zum anderen aus Wilsons Entscheidung, Gatsby zu ermorden. Der erste Teil endet mit Nicks aussagekräftigen Abschiedsworten an Gatsby, sodass diese Passage vor dem Hintergrund der bisherigen Handlung ausführlich behandelt werden sollte. Die Schülerinnen und Schüler lesen den ersten Teil des Kapitels (S. 104: 1–109: 22) und bearbeiten folgenden Arbeitsauftrag (evtl. als vorbereitende Hausaufgabe):

Read the first part of chapter 8 (up to page 109: 22).
This part is characterized by a very unconventional time structure. Illustrate the time structure by drawing a timeline that organizes this part in a less confusing way. Pay special attention to flashbacks and present time situations. Make notes on the actions that are presented for each time period.

Lösungsvorschlag

beginning of chapter 8–p. 104: 37: summer of 1922 (the night following Myrtle's death) Nick goes over to Gatsby's mansion.

p. 104: 38–107: 19: first flashback
October 1917: love affair between Gatsby and Daisy starts
late 1917: Gatsby goes to France on a cold fall day.
1918: Gatsby rises to the rank of major, is decorated for bravery in the battle.
fall of 1918: Daisy is gay again.
November 1918: the Armistice; Gatsby goes to Oxford.
middle of spring 1919: Tom Buchanan courts Daisy.
June 1919: Daisy marries Tom Buchanan; Gatsby is at Oxford.

p. 107: 20: summer of 1922 (the night after Myrtle's death)
Nick and Gatsby talk at Gatsby's house.

p. 107: 41–108: 24: second flashback
before August 1919: Tom and Daisy are still on their wedding trip; Gatsby revisits Louisville.

p. 108: 25–109: 22: summer of 1922 (the night after Myrtle's death)
Nick's last glimpse of Gatsby, when he leaves for New York.

Um die sinnstiftende Bedeutung zu erkennen, die Daisy für Gatsby darstellt, ist es notwendig, die verschiedenen Phasen zu erkennen, die Gatsbys Liebe durchläuft.
Als Einstieg wird den Schülerinnen und Schülern eine Liste mit Kollokationen präsentiert, zu denen sie ihnen bekannte Beispiele aus Filmen, Büchern etc. zuordnen sollen. Im Anschluss können noch passende Adjektive, die mit den Begriffen verknüpft werden, gesammelt werden, um den Wortschatz zu erweitern.

---

fall in love ■ lovebirds ■ unconditional love ■ unrequited love ■ love at first sight
■ happily ever after ■ one and only ■ Mr. Right ■ love triangle ■ made for each other
■ deep love ■ secret love ■ madly in love ■ to fall out of love ■ head over heels in love
■ true love ■ tender love ■ shallow love ■ blind lovers ■ sincere love …

In einem nächsten Schritt wenden die Schülerinnen und Schüler die verschiedenen Begriffe auf die Geschichte von Daisy und Gatsby an, indem sie sie in die Zeitleiste eintragen (siehe vorangegangene Hausaufgabe, S. 80) und mit Zitaten belegen.

> Describe the love of Daisy and Gatsby by matching the expressions with the development of their relationship as described in the flashbacks. Choose appropriate quotes from the novel to support your ideas.

Lösungsvorschlag

first phase:
Gatsby does not only love her but also her material world (her beautiful house with "its air of breathless intensity" (105: 3), with "its ripe mystery" (105: 5), because it is "beautiful and cool", "gay and radiant"; he loves the "shining motor cars", the dances, the fresh flowers etc. (105: 5ff.)
He is fascinated by her material wealth: "She vanished into her rich house, into her rich, full life" (105: 37), "Her porch was bright with the bought luxury of star-shine" (105: 42), "Gatsby was overwhelmingly aware of the youth and mystery that wealth imprisons and preserves, of the freshness of many clothes, and of Daisy, gleaming like silver, safe and proud above the hot struggles of the poor." (106: 1–4).
Daisy is also very desirable because there are many men who are interested in her. (105: 11f.)
= Gatsby is mostly attracted by Daisy's social and material background; he deceives her from the beginning (he is poor but doesn't show it; he acts as if has money and belongs to high society just like Daisy (insincere love, excited desire)

second phase:
Gatsby really falls in love with Daisy, "getting deeper in love every minute" (106: 9f.), "He felt married to her" (105: 38); their communication becomes tender and intense (106: 13ff.)
= true love, madly in love, tender love, romantic love, spiritual love etc.

third phase:
Gatsby loses Daisy because he is not there when she needs him most.
Daisy loves Gatsby, too, but she is not able to wait for Gatsby; she needs some form of orientation, stability and decision so she decides to marry Tom who is strong and dominant (106: 24ff.)

Folgende Schreibaufträge bieten sich im Anschluss an die Analyse der Liebesgeschichte an:

- Compose a letter that Gatsby might have sent to Daisy while he was fighting in World War I.
- Write a letter that Daisy might have written to Gatsby after her wedding with Tom.

In einem zweiten Schritt wird nun die Figur Gatsby anhand der doppeldeutigen Abschiedsworte Nicks abschließend analysiert. Dazu erhalten die Schülerinnen und Schüler *Copy 23* und bearbeiten die Arbeitsaufträge zunächst individuell, dann in Partnerarbeit.

Lösungsvorschlag

6. Nick's assessment of Gatsby is ambiguous: on the one hand he disapproves of the shady way Gatsby achieved his aims; on the other hand he believes that he still has some integrity left, unlike Tom and Daisy who he refers to as the 'damn bunch'. Gatsby's special quality in comparison to the other characters is not that he was free of corruption but that he was an idealist, that he possessed a dream.
Speculative: Nick was happy he said it because he never would have got another chance, since Gatsby was killed and that was the last time Nick saw him alive.

Read and respond

"Integrity is telling myself the truth. And honesty is telling the truth to other people." (Spencer Johnson)

Have you ever taken a stand that was unpopular and had to pay the price for that? What did you do? How did you feel afterward? What was the outcome? What did you learn from the experience? Write about this situation in one paragraph.

4.6 Discussion: Who is to blame for Gatsby's death?

Ausgehend von den Spekulationen über das Schicksal Gatsbys erarbeiten die Schülerinnen und Schüler nun den zweiten Teil des Kapitels 8. Dafür erhalten sie den Beginn und das Ende der Passage, in der sich Wilson für das Erschießen Gatsbys entscheidet. Idealerweise beginnt die Textarbeit gegen Ende einer Stunde, um das Schreiben der fehlenden Textmitte als Hausaufgabe aufgeben zu können. In der Folgestunde werden die Schülerergebnisse z. B. in einer *milling around activity* ausgetauscht. Dafür bewegen sich die Schülerinnen und Schüler frei im Raum und tauschen sich in einer bestimmten Zeit mit möglichst vielen Mitschülerinnen und Mitschülern über ihre Ideen aus. Im Anschluss können die Ergebnisse hinsichtlich bestimmter Kriterien bewertet werden (z. B. the most plausible, the craziest, the most interesting middle part).

What had happened to Gatsby and Wilson?
Write the middle part of this passage from Nick's point of view.

> "Now I want to go back a little and tell what happened at the garage after we left there the night before. [...] Until long after midnight a changing crowd lapped up against the front of the garage, while George Wilson rocked himself back and forth on the couch inside ..." (p. 110: 24 ff.)
>
> [...]
>
> "It was after we started with Gatsby toward the house that the gardener saw Wilson's body a little way off in the grass, and the holocaust was complete." (p. 114: 41 ff.)

Abschließend lesen die Schülerinnen und Schüler das Original und bearbeiten folgende *post-reading tasks*:

1. What does Wilson firmly believe happened to his wife? What clue(s) lead him to believe this?

   He is convinced that she was struck down on purpose by her lover; clues: he had found the leash and had threatened her to move away.

2. What does Nick mean when he says, "the holocaust was complete"? Consider the definition of the term 'holocaust'.

   A holocaust is the mass destruction of human life (innocent people).
   [the Holocaust: the killing of millions of Jews by the Nazis in the 1930s and 1940s]

3. What does Wilson imagine about the eyes of Dr. T.J. Eckleburg?

   Wilson really thinks the eyes of Dr. T.J. Eckleburg are the eyes of God watching them. He feels that God 'knows' everything.

Die interessante Frage, ob Wilson als Mörder die alleinige Schuld an Gatsbys Tod trägt, wird nun in einem 'Gerichtsprozess' diskutiert. Dazu versetzen sich die Schüler in verschiedene Rollen (Angeklagter Wilson, Richter, Zeugen, Staatsanwalt, Verteidiger, Jury) und bereiten sich auf der Grundlage der Lektüre auf eine Gerichtsverhandlung vor (siehe *Copy 24*).
Eine Gruppe von Schülerinnen und Schülern kann die Rolle der Jury übernehmen und nach dem Rollenspiel über ein Urteil abstimmen. Abschließend sollten die Schülerinnen und Schüler die Gelegenheit bekommen, ihre Rolle abzulegen und ihre eigene Meinung zu äußern.

The fight over Daisy

1. The quotes and expressions given below all refer to chapter 7 of *The Great Gatsby*. On your own, cut out the snippets and sort them into two piles: one with expressions you are sure you understand and can explain and the other pile with expression you need to clarify with a partner.

2. Now get together in pairs and discuss the cards from the second pile.

3. Now take one set of cards and arrange them in a way which you think shows best how they relate or interplay with each other.

4. Present your concept to your partner and explain it. Then listen to your partner's and agree on one concept that you both support. Be prepared to present your result to the rest of the class.

✂

"the whole cara-vansary had fallen in like a card house"	"His hand, trembling with his effort at self-control, bore to his lips the last of his glass of ale."	"You look so cool […] You always look so cool."	"The God damned coward! […] He didn't even stop his car."	"circus wagon"
"small investigation on this fellow"	lunch at the Buchanans' house	Plaza Hotel	"Your wife doesn't love you. She's never loved you. She loves me."	"You're revolting."
"her eyes wide with jealous terror"	"I'm going to get her away."	"natural intimacy"	"sacred vigil over nothing"	"Oh, you want too much!"

5. Chapter 7 is often described as a classical play in itself, made up of an exposition, a stage of rising action, a turning point and climax, as well as a stage of falling action and an ending. Check the definition of these literary terms on page 134 of your novel.
   Glue your snippets onto a big sheet of paper and mark the different stages in your concept using a different colour. Be prepared to explain your choices.

Writing practice: analysing symbolism

Take a close look at the model analysis given below.

1. **Structure: Compare the four paragraphs and describe their structure.**

2. **Language: Underline relevant phrases and expressions for writing an analysis of symbols used in a work of fiction. For future written assignments, make a list of all the relevant phrases and expressions.**

It has often been said that "rain and sunshine in novels are never accidental". Since there is no causal link between the weather and action, the weather clearly has a symbolic function. The reunion scene of Gatsby and Daisy that takes place in chapter 5 of the novel contains precise descriptions of the weather situation of that day and underlines the atmosphere and development of the plot.

The reunion scene is accompanied by rain. It is "pouring rain" when Gatsby makes his last inspection of Nick's house (p. 61: 35). Shortly before Daisy's arrival the rain changes to "damp mist" (p. 62: 18) but the rain soon starts again. The pouring rain outside reflects the atmosphere inside: the tension, the awkwardness of the situation. It is also a bad omen and their first date seems destined to be a failure.

Before Nick re-enters the house to find a happy couple, the sun breaks through (p. 65: 8). As soon as the sun starts to shine outside, the atmosphere inside has changed completely ("every vestige of embarrassment was gone", p. 65: 22). The change of weather, therefore, emphasizes the positive and relaxed situation.

During the rest of the meeting it rains again, with one significant exception: for a short time, some clouds are lit up by the sun and Daisy is anxious for Gatsby to witness that event: "Come here quick." (p. 68: 37) The sunlit clouds in the midst of the darkness are visible only for a very short time and, therefore, become a symbol of the very short moment of happiness they share.

3. **Now it's your turn! Write your own analysis of the symbolic use of weather in the first scene of chapter 7 (lunch scene). Make use of the relevant phrases and expressions as much as possible and follow the structure of the model analysis.**

Colours as symbols

One type of symbol that is particularly prevalent throughout the novel is colour. Colours have connotations, or additional meaning associated with them. These connotations can be crucial in deciphering the meaning and importance behind characters, images, or objects.

Re-read following pages of *The Great Gatsby* that all include references to various colours. Then complete the given tasks.

✂ -

WHITE

Take a look at chapter 1, pp. 10 + 19 and chapter 4, p. 55. Who/What is usually associated with the colour white? Find at least three examples from the text and explain the context.

Then compare your own personal initial associations of the colour with the connotations it has in the novel: Do you agree with the association? Why or why not? Explain your answer using examples from the text.

✂ -

GOLD; YELLOW

Take a look at chapter 4, p. 48 and chapter 2, p. 26. Who and what are associated with the colour gold or yellow? Find at least two examples from the text and explain the context.

How well does your list of associations work to describe the characters and objects linked with the colour? Explain your answer using examples from the text.

✂ -

GREEN

Take a look at chapter 6, p. 76, chapter 5, p. 68, and chapter 7, p. 97. Which objects are associated with the colour green? Find at least three examples from the text and explain the context.

Do you agree with the association between your ideas of the colour green and the depiction of the objects linked to the colour green? Why or why not? Explain your answer by using examples from the text.

✂ -

GREY

Take a look at chapter 2, p. 21 + 23, chapter 8, p. 112. Who and what are associated with the colour? Find at least three examples from the text and explain the context.

Compare your list of associations with the references to the colour in the text. Do you agree with the association? Why or why not? Explain your answer using examples from the text.

Evaluating Gatsby

1. Define integrity in one to two sentences.

2. Write down three guidelines for demonstrating integrity a) in and b) outside school.

3. Compare your ideas and discuss differences and similarities. Agree on one solution for both tasks.

4. Reread Nick's words of goodbye to Gatsby. Complete the table by writing down notes on the questions about the quote.

    'They're a rotten crowd,' I shouted across the lawn.
    'You're worth the whole damn bunch put together.'
    I've always been glad I said that. It was the only compliment I ever gave him,
    because I disapproved of him from the beginning to end. (p. 109: 7 ff.)

5. Then swap papers with your partner. Read his/her responses and comment on them by writing down some feedback, additional remarks etc. Do not speak but discuss your ideas silently. Use phrases for giving opinion.

6. Finally, write a paragraph that sums up your ideas. Make clear where you and your partner's interpretations differ.

My notes	My partner's comment
What is the context of the passage?	
Who is the 'bunch' Nick is referring to?	
What does he mean by his remark? Does he approve of Gatsby or not in the end?	
How does the theme of integrity apply to Gatsby?	
What do you think: why is Nick glad he said it?	

Putting a character on trial

Group tasks

Imagine George hasn't committed suicide but has been arrested by the police and is now put on trial for murdering Gatsby.
Is he really guilty of murder?
Is he the only one responsible for the tragedy?

Assign members of your group different parts to play in the trial.

judge:	Witnesses Nick:
Wilson (defendant):	Wilson's neighbour:
defence lawyer:	Daisy:
prosecutor:	Tom:

Make sure all testimonies stay true to the story as to what witnesses might say.

Use evidence and direct quotes from the novel in your testimonies.

Read through the common courtroom phrases given below and highlight the ones that suit your role. Make use of them as much as possible during your performance.

Common courtroom phrases

- Do you solemnly swear that the testimony you are about to give shall be the truth, the whole truth and nothing but the truth, so help you God?
- Please tell the court.
- Objection, Your Honour.
- Objection sustained/overruled.
- What, if anything, happened on that night?
- Take the witness stand.
- What was the first thing that attracted your attention?
- Your Honour, may I approach the witness?
- The people call John to the stand.
- Thank you, you're excused.
- Did anything unusual happen?
- Can you tell the jury …?
- Could you briefly describe …?
- You can answer the question.
- Are you familiar with this?
- Do you wish to say anything before sentence is imposed?
- Did you notice anything about (the envelope, etc.)?
- Have you reached a verdict?

Component 5

American dreams, American nightmares

5.1 The ideal of the American Dream

In Kapitel 9 werden zum einen die Biografien von Gatsby und Nick abgeschlossen, zum anderen erfolgt in den letzten beiden Absätzen des Romans eine explizite Verknüpfung von Gatsbys privatem Schicksal mit der amerikanischen Geschichte. Um diese letzten Zeilen, die zu den berühmtesten (und auch umstrittensten) Passagen in der amerikanischen Literatur zählen, verstehen zu können, ist ein Exkurs zur Idee des *American Dream* notwendig. Dies erfolgt zum einen anhand eines Sachtextes *(Copy 26)* zum amerikanischen Traum, zum anderen anhand eines Ausschnitts aus der Biografie Benjamin Franklins, der den amerikanischen Traum verkörpert und dessen Arbeitsethos Gatsby in seiner Jugend zu beeinflussen schien *(Copy 25)*.

Die beiden Materialien werden den Schülerinnen und Schülern zur vorbereitenden Lektüre ausgeteilt und zwar so, dass die eine Hälfte der Schülerinnen und Schülern nur *Copy 26*, die andere Hälfte *Copy 25* erhält. Im Unterricht informieren sich jeweils zwei Schülerinnen und Schüler gegenseitig über ihre Texte und bearbeiten dann gemeinsam folgende Frage:

> Benjamin Franklin: The man who invented the American Dream. Explain.

Zur vorherigen Absicherung der Arbeitsergebnisse bietet es sich auch an, dass sich vor dem Beginn der Austauschphase Schülerpaare mit den gleichen Ausgangstexten bilden. Am Schluss der Stunde muss sichergestellt werden, dass alle Schüler über grundlegende Kenntnisse des *American Dream* verfügen, da sie für den weiteren Verlauf der Unterrichtseinheit notwendig sind. Aus diesem Grund sollte auf eine ausreichende Sicherungsphase mit Tafelbild geachtet werden:

Lösungsvorschläge zu *Copy 25*

1. suitable adjectives: successful, eager, ambitious, intelligent, clever, hardworking, determined, enthusiastic, open-minded, earnest, industrious, …

2. paraphrasing of values: 1. not to eat or drink too much; 2. use speech carefully or to teach/learn; 3. organize one's life; 4. decide what to do, and then do it; 5. use only what you need; 6. work hard and use one's time well; 7. speak only the truth; 8. do one's duty to others and avoid doing wrong; 9. keep your temper; 10. keep one's mind and body clean; 11. remain calm even when there are problems; 12. use sex in moderation; 13. be modest and not show pride

Lösungsvorschläge zu *Copy 26*

	Belief in freedom	Belief in equality of opportunity	Belief in success
Historical meaning	• escape Old World, powers and control • government of the people, for the people and by the people	• everybody has the same chance of success • people are not equal, they have equal opportunities	• hard work leads to success, success is a sign of God's grace • pursuit of happiness: success through hard work
Qualities needed	• to be self-reliant, self-sufficient		• hard-working

In einer Vertiefungsphase können die Lebensmaximen von Franklin näher diskutiert werden. Diese Aufgabe eignet sich auch als Einstieg in eine Unterrichtsstunde zu „Benjamin Franklin", falls das unter 5.1 aufgelistete Material nicht arbeitsteilig eingesetzt wird.

a) Benjamin Franklin's maxims are still very well-known in the US. Discuss if they still apply in the 21st century.

b) The following proverbs were coined by Franklin. What do they mean? Do you agree with him?
   • Have you somewhat to do tomorrow, do it today.
   • Lost time is never found again.
   • Early to bed and early to rise makes a man healthy, wealthy and wise.
   • Not to oversee workmen, is to leave them your purse open.

Falls die Schüler das 9. Kapitel noch nicht gelesen haben, wird folgender Auszug präsentiert und erläutert. Ansonsten können die Schüler die Verknüpfung zwischen Gatsby und Franklin selbstständig herstellen und erhalten nur den Arbeitsauftrag.

Gatsby's father arrives for his son's funeral. While looking at his son's personal belongings he finds a book that includes some interesting hand-written notes …
Read p. 121: 35 to 122: 12.
Why does Mr Gatz show Nick Gatsby's schedule from his youth? What does this show you about the kind of person Gatsby was meant to be? Why do you think this was an important/unimportant part of the novel?

Lösungsvorschlag

Mr Gatz wanted Nick (and the reader) to see the kind of personal determination Gatsby had. He was meant to become something important, and always had the best intentions.

Read and respond

How do you define 'being a social success'? Think of your own personal definition and then draw up a list of advice on how to become a social success.

To be a social success you must: _____

Die Schüler lesen zu Hause Kapitel 9 und bearbeiten *Copy 27*.

5.2 "They are careless people!" – dramatic reading

Im Anschluss an den Exkurs zum *American Dream* erfolgt nun die Betrachtung der Schlussszenen, d.h. vor allem der Reaktionen der anderen Charaktere auf Gatsbys Tod. Dabei stehen Tom und Daisy Buchanan im Vordergrund. Zuvor muss allerdings das Textverständnis von Kapitel 9 *(Copy 27)* gesichert werden. Die Schülerinnen und Schüler vergleichen in Partnerarbeit ihre Ergebnisse und verfassen dann auf der Basis der Zitate eine mündliche Zusammenfassung des Kapitels. Die Zitate der Hausaufgabe können dabei als Stütze benutzt werden.

> **Lösungsvorschläge** *Copy 27*
>
> correct order of expressions:
> that I was responsible (115: 33)
> to have a feeling of defiance (116: 38)
> from a town in Minnesota (117: 26)
> to take the body West (118: 23)
> a pair of shoes (119: 15)
> getting sickantired (120: 2)
> right out of the gutter (120: 23)
> a ragged old copy of a book (121: 33)
> to go there by the hundreds (123: 11)
> That's my Middle West (123: 38)
> a night scene by El Greco (124: 14)
> She lay perfectly still (124: 33)
> crazy enough to kill me (125: 36)
> it seemed silly not to (126: 14)
> an obscene word (126: 36)
> green light at the end of Daisy's dock (127: 15)

Der Dialog zwischen Nick und Tom eignet sich sehr gut dazu, gefühlvolles und interpretierendes Lesen zu fördern – besonders auch, da Nick seine Gefühle nicht direkt artikuliert, sondern nur beschreibt. Diese ‚Kommunikationslücke' kann nun von den Schülerinnen und Schülern in einem *dramatic reading* ausgefüllt werden.
Zur Einstimmung werden Vermutungen gesammelt, wie ein solches Treffen nach den tragischen Ereignissen ablaufen würde:

> "One afternoon late in October I saw Tom Buchanan." (p. 125: 16) …
> Which questions would you like to ask Tom if you were in Nick's position?

Die Schülerinnen und Schüler erhalten dann **Copy 28** und bereiten sich in Dreiergruppen auf die Präsentation vor. Während der Präsentation sollte die Umsetzung von Nicks Kommentar zu Tom und Daisy nochmals hervorgehoben werden:

> How is Tom characterized in this scene?
>
> aggressive, restless, full of energy; but there is also a suggestion of self-pity and of cowardice ("He was crazy enough to kill me if I hadn't told him who owned the car.", p. 125: 36f.).

> Why does he call Daisy and Tom 'careless people'?
>
> Tom and Daisy cared only about themselves. When Daisy is put to the test to show her integrity, she and Tom run away to let Nick and others clean up after

them. Not only do they not attend Gatsby's funeral, but Tom and Daisy completely ignore and neglect the issue of Gatsby's death. What is more, Tom refuses to accept any kind of responsibilty in the events prior to the killing of Gatsby, and Wilson's suicide. Apparently, Daisy has not told Tom the truth about the night of the accident. Instead, they are busy moving into their new house, hiding behind their materialistic attitude and closing a door on the past.

Da Nick sich während des Gesprächs nur sehr zurückhaltend äußert (im Gegensatz zu seiner vernichtenden Kritik), bietet es sich an, den Dialog aus der Sicht eines eher extrovertierteren Erzählers neu zu verfassen:

As you can see, Nick remains very hesistant, almost unemotional during his encounter with Tom. Based on your knowledge about his convictions and beliefs, rewrite the ending of the dialogue so that Nick appears extremely emotional and expressive.

5.3 Eulogy on the Great (?) Gatsby

Vor dem Hintergrund der gesamten Handlung ist es nun möglich, Nicks Bemerkungen zu Gatsbys Schicksal zu Beginn des Romans zu verstehen und dazu kritisch Stellung zu nehmen. Zur Erinnerung wird das Zitat (S. 7: 33 – S. 8: 15) für alle sichtbar präsentiert und unter Berücksichtigung folgender Fragestellungen untersucht:

This quote is NOT taken from chapter 9. At which point does Nick express these thoughts? Describe the context in your own words.
Make a list of all the attributes that Nick uses to describe Gatsby.
What is meant by "the foul dust floated in the wake of his dreams"?

Lösungsvorschlag

- context: the quote is taken from the introductory pages of the novel. Nick reflects on the events that have already taken place and that he is about to narrate.
- attributes: idealistic, sensitive, gorgeous, hopeful, optimistic, romantic, ...
- Gatsby is seen as a victim, the only true 'dreamer' who is not wise or strong enough to see that Daisy is not worthy of his devotion, of his sacrifice.

Gatsbys Leben soll nun aus der Perspektive Nicks hinreichend gewürdigt werden. Dies erfolgt zum Kontext des Romans passend im Rahmen einer (Lob)Rede, die die Schülerinnen und Schüler für Nick für die Trauerfeier vorbereiten und dann halten sollen. Unterstützend erhalten die Schüler dafür *Copy 29*, auf der wesentliche Kriterien für den Aufbau einer Rede sowie Redemittel präsentiert werden.
Naturgemäß handelt es sich bei derartigen Reden um positive Würdigungen der Verstorbenen. Nach der Präsentation einiger Reden sollen die Schülerinnen und Schüler abschließend aber die Gelegenheit bekommen, Nicks Haltung in Bezug auf Gatsby kritisch zu beurteilen.

Do you think Gatsby is worthy of Nick's overall positive evaluation?

worthy	unworthy
he is a dedicated, determined dreamer; faithful to his dream to the very end	he is a bootlegger, a crook; materialistic; tries to produce the riches he thinks necessary by shady, even criminal means (lacks financial background); corrupt; false belief that a noble purpose justifies all means.
has a loyal heart (takes the blame for killing Myrtle; remains outside Daisy's window to make sure that she is not hurt)	
has the extraordinary ability to transform his dreams and hopes into reality strong belief in American Dream of success: determined that if he only stuck to his plan he could achieve whatever he set out to accomplish	

5.4 From dream to nightmare: the decline of the American Dream in the 1920s

Zu Beginn werden wesentliche Aspekte des *American Dream* reaktiviert, um sie dem Gesellschaftsbild, das Fitzgerald zeichnet, gegenüberzustellen. Dies erfolgt über einen Auszug aus dem Schlusskapitel des Romans (S. 126: 34–127: 12) in Verbindung mit folgender Fragestellung:

> **Who is meant by the "Dutch sailors"? What do they dream of?**
>
> European immigrants in general, coming to North America to escape political, religious persecution and poverty, to live the American Dream of freedom, liberty, pursuit of happiness

Die Schüler bilden im Anschluss Gruppen, in denen Experten zu den Hauptcharakteren des Romans vertreten sind (siehe **Component 2**). Die *character sheets* sollten nun vollständig ausgefüllt sein und für die Bearbeitung der Aufgabenstellung verwendet werden. Folgende Trends und Missstände sollten die Gruppen von den Charakteren des Romans ableiten:

> **predominant values and flaws:**
>
> - unrestrained desire for money and pleasure
>   (examples: opulent parties that Gatsby throws every Saturday night; Daisy's materialistic lifestyle; Gatsby's dream of loving Daisy ruined by differences in their social status; Nick's move to the East to make a quick fortune; Myrtle's effort to climb the social ladder by means of her love affair with Tom)
> - crime and corruption
>   (Wolfshiem; Gatsby: resorting to crime in order to make enough money to impress Daisy)
> - adultery and cheating
>   (Tom, Daisy and Myrtle betray their spouses; Jordan cheats at golf in order to advance her career)
> - unequal distribution of material wealth
>   (society split into the very rich – Gatsby, the Buchanans – and the very poor – the Wilsons)
> - lack of purpose
>   (expressed by the Buchanans who seem to live for the moment only)
> - lack of concern for other people
>   (shown by the Buchanans: simply move to a new house rather than attending Gatsby's funeral)

conclusion:

society of the 1920s depicted in *The Great Gatsby* has lost its way, has become a shallow, materialistic nation, and is therefore far removed from the ideals of the American Dream

→ bleak and pessimistic view on America's future

Im Mittelpunkt des letzten Unterrichtsschrittes müssen die berühmten Abschlussworte Nicks stehen, die das Schicksal Gatsbys mit der Idee und der Realität des amerikanischen Traums verknüpfen. Die Schülerinnen und Schüler erhalten dafür **Copy 30**, auf der die Abschlussworte präsentiert werden; allerdings sind Lücken eingefügt, in denen die Schüler ihre Ideen und Assoziationen zu Fragen notieren. Das Zitat wird vom Lehrer (oder auch von einem Schüler) Stück für Stück vorgetragen, vor jeder Lücke erhalten die Schülerinnen und Schüler einen zum Gelesenen passenden Auftrag (siehe unten). Auf diese Weise setzen sich die Schülerinnen und Schüler nicht nur kreativ mit dem Text auseinander, indem sie Leerstellen füllen, sondern es werden nochmals wichtige Aspekte und Zusammenhänge wiederholt. Folgenden Arbeitsaufträge wären denkbar:

How did Gatsby feel at this time? Write that down.

He had come a long way to this blue lawn, and his dream must have seemed so close that he could hardly fail to grasp it.

Write down what he had done to be so close to his dream.

He did not know that it was already behind him somewhere back in the vast obscurity beyond the city, where the dark fields of the republic rolled under the night.

How would you explain to him that his dream is not going to come true?

Gatsby believed in the green light, the orgiastic future that year by year recedes before us.

Who is US?

It eluded us then, but that's no matter – tomorrow we will run faster, stretch out our arms farther … And one fine morning -

Why will we continue trying to live a dream?

So we beat on, boats against the current, borne back ceaselessly into the past.

Will we ever be successful?

Abschließend erhalten die Schülerinnen und Schüler Gelegenheit, ihre Notizen zu vervollständigen und zusammenhängend vorzutragen. Da diese letzten Zeilen von Bildern, Symbolen und Assoziationen dominiert werden, ist es auf der Basis des Textverständnisses nun möglich, kreativ mit dem Zitat umzugehen, indem die Passage in ein Bild oder eine Collage umgewandelt wird:

Based on the final lines, draw a picture or design a collage that illustrates the link between

Gatsby – the original American Dream – the present situation of mankind

according to the author.

Benjamin Franklin: The way to wealth

With less than three years of formal schooling, Benjamin Franklin (1706–1790), the fifteenth child of a poor candle maker, taught himself almost everything he knew. He took the initiative of learning
5 French, German, Italian, Latin, and Spanish. He taught himself how to play the guitar, violin and harp. He made himself an influential author and editor. He started a successful printing business, newspaper, and magazine. On his eight trans-Atlan-
10 tic crossings, Franklin made measurements that helped chart the Gulf Stream. He was most famous, of course, for his experiments with electricity, especially lightning. His lightning rod helped banish the terror of thunderstorms. Franklin had more to do
15 with founding the American republic than anyone else. He was a member of the committee that drafted the *Declaration of Independence* and he served as America's representative in France throughout the American War of Independence. After the Revolu-
20 tion, Franklin participated in the drafting of the US Constitution. Additionally, he has written several essays on how to achieve economic success and social upward mobility. One of his most renowned essays is *The Way to Wealth*. Here he specifically gave advice
25 on how to become successful and thriving. As prescribed by Franklin there are certain virtues one has to possess, if he or she wants to be successful in life.

1. Temperance
Eat not to Dulness. Drink not to Elevation.
2. Silence
Speak not but what may benefit others or yourself.
Avoid trifling Conversation.
3. Order
Let all your Things have their Places. Let each Part
of your Business have its Time.
4. Resolution.
Resolve to Perform what you ought. Perform
without fail what you resolve.
5. Frugality
Make no Expence but to do good to others or yourself: i.e., Waste nothing.
6. Industry
Lose no Time. Be always employ'd in something
useful. Cut off all unnecessary Actions.
7. Sincerity
Use no hurtful Deceit.
Think innocently and justly; and, if you speak,
speak accordingly.
8. Justice
Wrong none, by doing injuries or omitting the
Benefits that are your Duty.
9. Moderation
Avoid Extremes. Forbear resenting Injuries so much
as you think they deserve.
10. Cleanliness
Tolerate no Uncleanness in Body, Clothes or Habitation.
11. Tranquility
Be not disturbed at Trifles, or at Accidents common
or unavoidable.
12. Chastity
Rarely use Venery but for Health or Offspring;
Never to Dulness, Weakness, or the Injury of your
own or another's Peace or Reputation.
13. Humility
Imitate Jesus and Socrates.

Benjamin Franklin, The Way to Wealth, 1758

1. Read the text on Benjamin Franklin's life thoroughly. Find at least five suitable adjectives that describe his character.

2. Define in your own words each of the thirteen virtues.

The ideal of the American Dream

What is it that has lured tens of millions of people from every nation to the shores of the United States? This question was asked by the historian James Truslow Adams in the 1930s. His answer was the "American Dream", a set of beliefs, or sometimes called "core values", that is the foundation of American society:

Belief in freedom
Most of the earliest colonists came to the New World in the hope of escaping from the controls exercised in the Old World by monarchs, the church, and the autocratic governments in general. By sharply limiting the possible misuse of authority, the Founding Fathers created a climate of freedom for every individual citizen. This meant that the American way of life became firmly associated with the notion of individual freedom. There would be no more outside interference with the private pursuit of happiness in America. That means, however, that the individual must learn to be self-sufficient and rely on himself in any thing he is doing – or risk losing his freedom.

Belief in equality of opportunity
The conception of the fundamental equality of all people has been the most influential of all American ideals. It is essential that what Americans mean by equality of opportunity is not that everybody is – or should be – equal, but that each individual should have an equal chance to success. Everyone is supposed to have as good a chance as everyone else to achieve wealth by his own efforts.

Belief in success
The belief in equality of opportunity is closely related to the belief in success, a belief which has its roots in early American history. The early settlers undoubtedly thought of themselves as God's chosen people. The American attitude to work was formed by the Puritan work ethic which guided people's attitude towards the "pursuit of happiness", one of the main tenets of the Constitution. The belief that success was an outward sign of God's grace found many followers, who desired to achieve success through hard work.

1. Explain the historical meaning of the "core values"!

2. Which qualities were needed to make the American Dream come true? Fill out the chart:

	Belief in freedom	Belief in equality of opportunity	Belief in success
Historical meaning			
Qualities needed			

While-reading task: chapter 9

Find the following words and phrases in chapter 9 and write down the complete sentence in which they are used. Then arrange the sentences in the order in which they are used in the original.

She lay perfectly still …

That's my Middle West …

… that I was responsible …

… an obscene word …

… green light at the end of Daisy's dock …

… to have a feeling of defiance …

… from a town in Minnesota …

… to take the body West …

… a ragged old Copy of a book …

… to go there by the hundreds …

… a pair of shoes …

… getting sickantired …

… right out of the gutter …

… a night scene by El Greco …

… crazy enough to kill me …

… it seemed silly not to …

Dramatic reading

1. Work in groups of three.

2. Reread the conversation between Nick and Tom Buchanan after Gatsby's funeral (p. 125: 16–p. 126: 17). Through discussion, work out answers to the following questions:

   ● What is each character's state of mind before the meeting? How are they feeling?
   ● How they feel when they first recognize each other?
   ● Which emotions do they go through while they are speaking to each other?
   ● What is going to happen next after they depart?
   ● How do the characters sound when they speak?

3. Using your answers to the questions, prepare a dramatized reading of the dialogue – trying to make clear what the situation is, who the characters are and what the relationship between them is. Two of the group members will perform the dialogue; the third member will prepare a short introduction to the scene and explanation at the end of the presentation.

4. How should the two characters sound? Based on your interpretation of the passage, …
   ● … underline any words you think should be given full stress,
   ● … mark with a V any places where you think there should be a pause,
   ● … mark any words or phrases you feel should be spoken in a special way: softly, sarcastically, etc. The expressions in the box given below might be helpful.

angry ■ annoyed ■ anxious ■ bored ■ concerned ■ confused ■ cross
■ depressed ■ devastated ■ embarrassed ■ excited ■ happy ■ impatient
■ indifferent ■ jealous ■ miserable ■ nervous ■ overjoyed ■ proud
■ relaxed ■ relieved ■ resigned ■ sad ■ shocked ■ shy ■ surprised ■ tense
■ unhappy ■ upset ■ worried

5. Nick does not respond to Tom's remarks. Based on the original text invent Nick's final remark to Tom before they depart and include it in your presentation. Be prepared to explain your choice.

6. Practise your performance two – three times so that you are able to read out the scene without looking at the text.

How to write a eulogy

A eulogy is a formal speech delivered at a funeral, in praise of the deceased. It's usually delivered by a relative or close friend of the deceased, or sometimes by a priest, minister or rabbi. There is no one right way to write a eulogy. Biographical information is part of the eulogy, but not the most important component. The eulogy should primarily express how you feel about the person you're eulogizing, as well as how the person affected you and others. It should be a heartfelt, personal and gracious sendoff for the deceased.

On the occasion of Gatsby's funeral Nick is to make a short speech in his honour. Write the speech for him.

How to write your eulogy:
Collect those qualities that are characteristic of him. Summarize his three greatest qualities. Select one that you will talk about in detail.
Retell what he taught you, what he enjoyed in life and why you will miss him.
Talk about one event described in the novel and retell it as an anecdote.
Think of who else is going to be there and think of a way to address them.
End your eulogy on one praising word.

Useful phrases:
- For those of you who do not know me, my name is … and I am
- It is with great sadness that I stand in front of you today to celebrate the life of …
- …. life was taken away from us too soon and it is hard to understand why …
- Today let's celebrate his life and remember all of the remarkable things … accomplished.

Talking to the text

The following extract is the final passage of the novel. It is one of the most famous passages in American literature – why? Many experts argue that in these lines, Gatsby and his dream are linked with the original American Dream and with the present human condition. Check yourself if you can understand the connection.

Below you find a Copy of Nick's final words at the very end of the novel (p. 127: 13 ff.). The text will be read out to you step by step. After each gap, there will be a question or task for you. Write down your ideas in note form as quickly as you can.

And as I sat there brooding on the old, unknown world, I thought of Gatsby's wonder when he first picked out the green light at the end of Daisy's dock.

He had come a long way to this blue lawn, and his dream must have seemed so close that he could hardly fail to grasp it.

He did not know that it was already behind him somewhere back in the vast obscurity beyond the city, where the dark fields of the republic rolled under the night.

Gatsby believed in the green light, the orgastic future that year by year recedes before us.

It eluded us then, but that's no matter – tomorrow we will run faster, stretch out our arms farther … And one fine morning -

So we beat on, boats against the current, borne back ceaselessly into the past.

Component 6

Post-reading activities

6.1 Creative writing ideas

Folgende kreative Schreibaufträge bieten sich im Anschluss an die Lektüre an und erfordern unterschiedliche Textformate, die je nach Schwerpunktsetzung für die konkrete Unterrichtssituation ausgewählt werden können:

1. Write an alternate ending to the novel. What would have happened if …
   … Gatsby had not been killed?
   … George Wilson had not committed suicide?
   … Daisy had left Tom for Gatsby?
   What happens next? You choose the point at which the story changes and what happens to each character.

2. Conduct an interview with either Tom or Daisy. Write at least 10 questions that will give the character a chance to tell his or her story from his or her point of view. You may ask questions, challenge a situation, express a complaint, or make a suggestion. Then answer the questions in the persona you chose.

3. Create a frontpage of a newspaper in which the deaths of Myrtle, Gatsby and George Wilson are reported. Before you write, read an issue of a current American newspaper for ideas on format, style, and layout. Note the type of language and word choice used in newspaper writing. You may include pictures.

4. Change perspective: how might the novel have been different if the story had been told from the 3rd-person point of view, or even from the point of view of another character, such as Daisy, Myrtle, or even George Wilson?

6.2 The structure of the plot – a gallery walk

Vor dem Hintergrund des gesamten Romans bietet es sich an, den Handlungsaufbau zu analysieren, indem die Schülerinnen und Schüler nach einer kurzen Einführung in die wesentlichen Strukturelemente diese an der Romanhandlung festmachen, grafisch darstellen und anschließend präsentieren.
Zur Vorbereitung auf die Präsentationsphase gestaltet jede Gruppe ein Plakat, auf dem die Handlungsstruktur anschaulich dargestellt wird. Um die mündlichen Präsentationskompetenzen möglichst vieler Schülerinnen und Schüler zu fördern, werden sie in der letzten Phase in neuen Gruppen zusammengesetzt, sodass sich in jeder Gruppe Vertreter aller Ausgangsgruppen befinden.
Nun findet ein „Durchgang durch die Galerie" statt, d. h. die Gruppen verteilen sich zu Beginn auf die im Klassenzimmer aufgehängten Plakate, die dann vom jeweiligen „Experten" (der Schüler oder die Schülerin, der an der Gestaltung beteiligt war) vorgestellt werden. Die Gruppen bewegen sich nun von Plakat zu Plakat und diskutieren Gemeinsamkeiten und Unterschiede der Ergebnisse.

Lösungsvorschlag

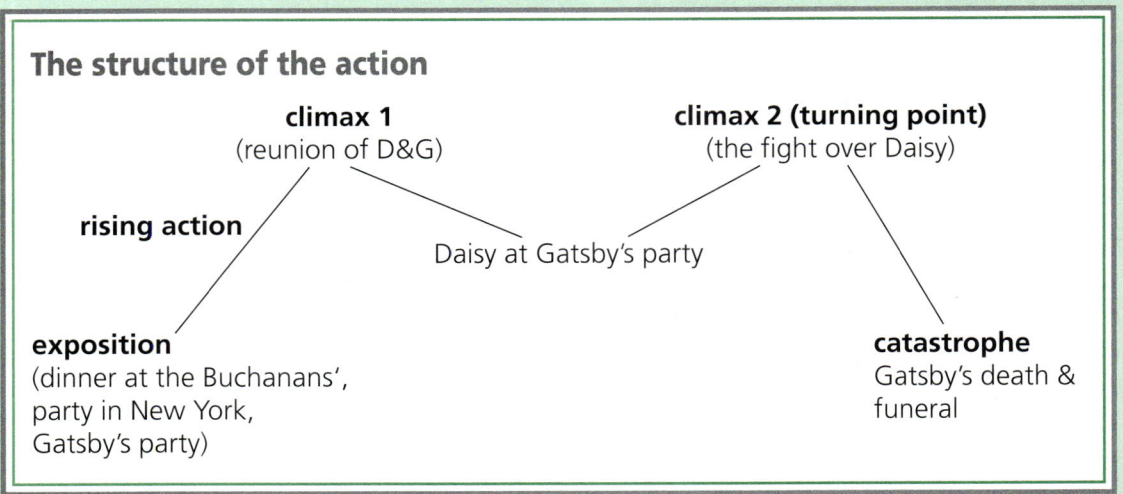

The structure of the action

climax 1
(reunion of D&G)

climax 2 (turning point)
(the fight over Daisy)

rising action

Daisy at Gatsby's party

exposition
(dinner at the Buchanans',
party in New York,
Gatsby's party)

catastrophe
Gatsby's death &
funeral

6.3 Screen adaption

Es ist natürlich sinnvoll, eine der Filmversionen des Romans im Unterricht zu sehen, mit dem Roman zu vergleichen, Unterschiede zu bewerten und Filmkritiken zu studieren. Eine interessante und kreative Aufgabe ist es aber auch, die Schülerinnen und Schüler anzuleiten, eigene Ideen zu entwickeln, wie bestimmte Schlüsselszenen filmisch effektiv umgesetzt werden sollten.

Dazu informieren sich die Schülerinnen und Schüler vorab (wenn nicht bereits erfolgt) über ausgewählte Begriffe der Filmsprache *(field sizes, point of view, camera angles, camera movement, sound, special effects, etc.)*. Es ist für die Übung allerdings nicht notwendig, über umfassende und professionelle Kenntnisse des Filmemachens zu verfügen: Die Schülerinnen und Schüler sollen viel mehr befähigt werden, ihre eigenen Vorstellungen und Bilder konkret umzusetzen.

Folgende Schlüsselszenen bieten sich für eine filmische Umsetzung an:

- fight at the Plaza Hotel
- one of Gatsby's legendary summer parties
- the reunion of Daisy and Gatsby at his mansion
- lunch at the Buchanans' before they all go to New York City

Es ist sinnvoll, wenn mehrere Schülergruppen dieselbe Szene wählen, damit im Anschluss verschiedene Versionen verglichen und diskutiert werden können. Die Schülerinnen und Schüler erhalten *Copy 31* und bearbeiten die Arbeitsaufträge für ihre ausgewählte Szene. Es wäre günstig, die ersten beiden Arbeitsaufträge als Hausaufgabe bearbeiten zu lassen. Die Schülerinnen und Schüler notieren dafür ihre eigenen Ideen, diskutieren im Unterricht verschiedene Möglichkeiten und einigen sich dann auf eine Gruppenentscheidung.

Folgende Fragen eignen sich für eine Feedbackrunde im Anschluss an die Vorstellung:

- How different were the versions?
- Were there any major differences of interpretation?
- What details made for more effective scripts (for example, sound effects, camera shots, etc.)?
- How did this activity help you to understand the story better?

Nun sollte der Film natürlich auch gezeigt werden und mit den Ideen der Schülerinnen und Schüler verglichen werden. Ein Vergleich zwischen Roman und Film erfolgt dann unter folgenden möglichen Fragestellungen, die die Schüler arbeitsteilig übernehmen:

- How well do you think was the cast of characters chosen?
- Which parts of the book were left out? Which scenes were added to the film version?
- Try to explain the director's decision to leave out or add certain aspects. Do you agree with the director's decisions?
- How well did the director capture the important themes/ideas of the novel?
- Could you notice any simplifications? Can you think of a reason for the director's decision?
- In which way are thoughts of individual characters expressed in the film?
- Compare the beginning and ending of the novel and the film.
- Which do you like better, the film or the novel? Why?
- Which is your favourite scene? Why?
- Was the dialogue close to the novel or loosely based on the novel?

6.4 The autobiographical background of the novel

Falls die Informationen zum Autor auf S. 128/129 der Textausgabe noch nicht behandelt wurden, können sie nun nach der Lektüre des Romans eingesetzt werden, um Parallelen zwischen der Biografie Fitzgeralds und der Romanhandlung herzustellen. Folgende Arbeitsaufträge begleiten den Leseprozess:

In what sense is *The Great Gatsby* an autobiographical novel?
Make a timeline that illustrates major events in the author's life.
Mark similarities and/or differences between the two lives – Fitzgerald's and Gatsby's. Autobiographical elements include:

- The Fitzgeralds lived in Long Island during the early 1920s and gave and went to parties similar to Gatsby's.
- Fitzgerald loved his wife more than anything in his life and yet he hated her for destroying his talent (= writing).
- Daisy Buchanan resembles Zelda (looks, behaviour, materialistic attitude, social background).
- Like Jay Gatsby, the Midwestern Fitzgerald was an outsider with no money and no respectable family.
- As a young man, he enlisted in the army.
- After the War he was determined to be a famous writer und worked hard to make his dream come true (unlike Gatsby, more like Nick?)
- Just as Gatsby's love for Daisy drove him to tragedy, Fitzgerald's love for Zelda occupied more and more of his time; she destroyed his dream of becoming a successful novelist.

Folgende abschließende Schreibaufträge sind nun denkbar:

After having read about the author's life, which parts of the film are easier for you to understand now?

Does Fitzgerald write more of himself into the character of Nick or the character of Gatsby? Or are the author's qualities found in both characters?

Screen adaption

Work in groups. It is your task to prepare a film version of one important scene of the novel *The Great Gatsby*.

1. Choose one of the given scenes.

2. Read 'your' passage several times and read it as if you were watching a film of the action.

3. Copy the following table onto a large sheet of paper and discuss various ideas. Complete the table by making notes on your group decision.

   - In the first column, you write the actual words from the text which suggest a camera shot.
   - In the middle column, you describe the camera movement.
   - In the last column, you note the dialogue and/or sound effects which accompany each shot.

Words in the text	Camera movement	Words that are spoken/ sound effects

4. Discuss the following aspects in your group and sum up your decision on a separate poster:

   - You have the choice of any actors and actresses to play in your film version. Who would you cast in which roles and why?

   - What clothes should they wear?

   - What kind of setting would you choose? Give a precise description.

   - Which song would you choose as a soundtrack for your modern movie version of *The Great Gatsby*? Explain your choice.

Focus on language

Im Fokus des letzten *Components* steht nun nicht mehr primär der Inhalt des Romans, sondern die sprachliche Ausdrucksfähigkeit, mit der die Schülerinnen und Schüler über den Inhalt sprechen und schreiben sollen. Anhand von ausgewählten Übungen wird zum einen der neue Wortschatz gefestigt und im Kontext des Romans angewendet. Zum anderen werden Möglichkeiten angeboten, die stilistische Ausdrucksweise schrittweise zu verbessern. Alle Kopiervorlagen sind natürlich flexibel je nach Leistungsstand und Bedürfnissen der Schülerinnen und Schüler einsetzbar. Da die Materialien als Ergänzung zum Literaturunterricht gelten, ist jeweils angegeben, auf welches Kapitel des Romans sich die Übungen beziehen bzw. nach welchem Kapitel diese eingesetzt werden können.

Übersicht der Kopiervorlagen:

Focus on style
Copy 32   Connecting your ideas (chapter 1)
Copy 33   Stressing your message (chapter 3)
Copy 34   Avoiding repetition (chapter 5)
Copy 35   Using participle clauses (chapter 6)

Focus on words
Copy 36   Brain 28 (chapter 2 & 3)
Copy 37   Adjectives (chapter 4)
Copy 38   Vocabulary replacement (chapter 7 & 8)

Lösungsvorschläge

Copy 32: Connecting your ideas (chapter 1)

A
above all → to emphasize; such as → to give examples; finally → to show a sequence; due to → to show cause and effect; furthermore → to add information; as well as → to compare; as a result → to draw a conclusion; whereas → to show differences; obviously → to emphasize

B
1. The opening paragraphs show us a lot about Nick and his attitude toward life in the East. <u>Besides</u>, it is said what he thinks about Gatsby.
2. Nick introduces himself to the reader as a young man from the Midwest who has come East <u>in order to learn/because</u> he intends to learn the bond business.
3. If you read closely, you'll see that Nick has contrasting feelings towards his neighbour: <u>on the one hand</u> he admires him <u>but, on the other hand,</u> he is critical of him.
4. <u>Since</u> he dislikes his former life in the Midwest he moves to the East.
5. West Egg is the home of the people who don't have the family background or the money to live in fashionable East Egg. <u>Evidently,</u> East Egg is like a fairyland.

6. Daisy is Nick's cousin. <u>That's why</u> he has the credentials to visit East Egg.
7. The Buchanans' house is a beautiful "Gregorgian Colonial Mansion" over-looking the bay. <u>Apparently,</u> its owner is proud of his possessions.

C

1. <u>As</u> Nick arrives at his cousin's mansion he also meets Jordan, a professional golfer and girlhood friend of Daisy's.
2. Jordan Baker yawns more than once in this very first scene. She is <u>apparently</u> quite bored and discontent.
3. <u>As</u> the foursome lounges around the estate, they discuss the day's most pressing matters, <u>including</u> what to do on the longest day of the year and other such shallow topics.
4. Tom talks about a book he has read advocating that the white race beat down the coloured races <u>first</u> <u>before</u> they rise up and <u>then</u> overcome the whites.
5. His wife seems not to understand what Tom is talking about <u>because</u> she teases him about the big words in the book.
6. <u>When</u> Tom takes a phone call, Jordan informs Nick that Tom's mistress is on the line.
7. Tom is known for his infidelities and <u>thus</u> he makes no pretence to cover up his affair.
8. Jordan is playing a tournament the next day <u>so that</u> the evening ends early.
9. <u>Before</u> Nick returns home, Tom and Daisy hint that they would welcome his attentions to Jordan Baker during the summer.

Copy 33: Stressing your message (chapter 3)

A

1. inversion
2. the construction *What … is/was …*
3. emphatic verb form
4. the construction *It is/was …*
5. a short sentence after a series of longer ones
6. a question after a series of statements
7. adverb of degree (above all)

B

1. What I found astonishing was the quantity of alcohol that was served in un-limited quantities in diverse forms – in spite of Prohibition!
2. Everything was particularly more modern, more colourful, more significant, more luxurious than anything I had ever seen.
3. For a long time I felt particularly attracted to the women: they danced all by themselves or took musical instruments from the orchestra.
4. There were elderly men and chorus girls, a group of young Englishmen, mar-ried couples – but where was the host?
5. Not only had the guests not been invited. They just went there and left chaos in their wake.
6. Most guests do not seem to care about the host. They do care about having fun though!
7. Hardly did I talk to a guest eye to eye. I was too distracted by the coloured lights, the buffet tables, the floating rounds of cocktails …
8. It was a bizarre car accident, the consequence of careless, drunken driving, that ended the party.

Copy 34: Avoiding repetition (chapter 5)

Upon arriving in West Egg, Nick finds all the lights in Gatsby's house blazing and Gatsby himself is walking toward him across the lawn. Gatsby invites Nick to go to Coney Island. When Nick turns him down, Gatsby invites Nick for a swim in the pool which he hasn't used all summer. Nick agrees to invite Daisy over. Gatsby suggests waiting a few days so that he can get Nick's grass cut. Then he offers Nick some money but Nick turns Gatsby down.
The big day arrives and it is raining. Gatsby is so nervous that he can hardly function. He has not slept. He is as pale as a high school boy on his first date. Life with Daisy in Louisville was so wonderful five years before; now he is terrified that even if Daisy should agree to renew their relationship, it won't be the same. Daisy arrives looking absolutely beautiful in a three-cornered lavender hat. She is dying to know why Nick has invited her over. Nick takes Daisy inside, thinking that Gatsby is waiting for her. But the room is empty …

Copy 35: Using participle clauses (chapter 6)

Die Lösungssätze von Schüler A sind automatisch die Lösungssätze von Schüler B und umgekehrt.

Copy 37: Adjectives (chapter 4)

1.
positive: gratified, frank, splendid, gorgeous, generous, hospitable, hilarious
negative: strained, offended, scornful, sombre, disconcerting
both: modest, roaring, inevitable

2.
greedy; respectful or polite; serious or grave; doubtful; pretentious or immodest; dishonest and indirect; unsatisfied

3.
roaring – loud and exciting; offended – angry and insulted; strained – troubled and disturbed; disconcerting – tense and worried; hilarious – entertaining; splendid – marvellous

Copy 38: Vocabulary/replacement (chapter 7 & 8)

1. I'm <u>relieved</u> because nobody was hurt in the accident.
2. It was quite <u>presumptuous</u> of my neighbour to assume that she was invited to our party even though she had not received an invitation.
3. The detective gave a shocking report on the <u>deranged</u> serial killer who stalked college students.
4. She opened her eyes and <u>exclaimed</u>, "It isn't fair".
5. Dreaming of her <u>sensuous</u> lips, he was unable to concentrate on the lecturer's words.
6. The sun was shining brightly and there was a mild breeze coming from the ocean. I was <u>tempted to</u> take the day off, even though I had clients waiting for me at my office.
7. I don't want to <u>bother</u> her with my problems at the moment. She looks too tired.
8. A <u>revolting</u> smell was in the air when she opened the door to her apartment.

9. Even though he already owned jewelry worth thousands of dollars, he stared at her diamonds with <u>greedy</u> eyes.

10. I am sure he'll come to our party if you persuade him.

11. She has never talked about her <u>precious</u> daughter before.

12. Police are <u>investigating</u> possible links between the murders.

13. After the young man ran into her, she realized that he was not sorry but acting with <u>malice</u>.

Connecting your ideas (chapter 1)

In order to make your writing flow and interesting to read, you need to connect your sentences by employing different linking words.

A Here is a list of quite useful linking words. Put the expressions into the correct category by writing them into the boxes.

> above all ■ such as ■ finally ■ due to ■ furthermore
> ■ as well as ■ as a result ■ whereas ■ obviously

To give examples for example – for instance – e.g. – i.e. – including – ...	**To compare** like – in the same way – similarly – compared to/with – ...
To emphasize in particular – especially – indeed – notably – apparently – evidently – actually – ...	**To show differences** although – despite – in spite of – neither ... nor – on the one hand ... on the other hand – however – ...
To show cause and effect because – consequently – since – for this reason – so that – thus – as a result – ...	**To add information** in addition – moreover – besides – apart from – ... , too – ...
To show a sequence first – then – next – meanwhile – afterwards – second(ly) – while – ...	**To draw a conclusion** to sum up – to conclude – all in all – in brief – therefore – in other words – ...

B The following sentences are rather short. Connect the two sentences by using suitable linking words from the list above.

1. The opening paragraphs show us a lot about Nick and his attitude toward life in the East. It is said what he thinks about Gatsby.

2. Nick introduces himself to the reader as a young man from the Midwest. He has come East to learn the bond business.

3. If you read closely, you'll see that Nick has contrasting feelings towards his neighbour: He admires him. He is critical of him.

4. He dislikes his former life in the Midwest. He moves to the East.

5. West Egg is the home of the people who don't have the family background or the money to live in fashionable East Egg. East Egg is like a fairyland.

6. Daisy is Nick's cousin. He has the credentials to visit East Egg.

7. The Buchanans' house is a beautiful "Gregorgian Colonial Mansion" overlooking the bay. Its owner is proud of his possessions.

C Reread the passage of chapter 1 in which Nick is having dinner with the Buchanans. Sum up the events of that evening in seven sentences using suitable linking words.

Stressing your message (chapter 3)

The techniques given below can all be used to stress the important parts of your sentences:

- emphatic verb forms *(e.g. do/does/did + infinitive)*
- adverbs of degree *(e.g. especially, particularly)*
- the construction *It is/was …*
- inversion (constructions *e.g. Hardly/Not only + auxiliary + subject + infinitive*)
- the construction *What … is/was …*
- *a short sentence* after a series of longer sentences
- *a question* after a series of statements

A Take a look at the sentences below and identify the emphatic devices being used. Say what ideas or elements in the sentences are being stressed.

1. Never before had Nick seen such a spiritless and pitiful man such as George Wilson.

2. What Myrtle Wilson longed for the most was luxury and admiration.

3. Even though they live in poverty, it has to be acknowledged that Wilson does love and adore his energetic and sensuous wife.

4. It was in the Valley of Ashes that Nick first meets Tom's mistress, Myrtle Wilson.

5. The six people spend the afternoon at Tom's apartment in New York City in a haze of drunkenness. As the afternoon wears on and she becomes increasingly intoxicated, Myrtle gets more and more outspoken about her personal situation in life, her marriage, her impassioned first meeting with Tom and, finally, Tom's marriage. Upon mentioning Daisy's name, Myrtle becomes enraged, shouting "Daisy" at the top of her lungs. Suddenly Tom hits her with his open hand.

6. Everyone could see that they did not get along well, that they had lost any kind of passion long ago, if it had ever been there, and that she looked down on him. So why did she not leave her husband?

7. She was a sensuous woman in her mid thirties who had the energy her husband lacked. Above all, she had a fire inside her that had drawn her to Tom Buchanan as a lover who can take her away from the grey and empty prison of the Valley of Ashes.

B You have just read chapter 3 of the novel. Put yourself into Myrtle's position and imagine you were invited to Gatsby's party. Describe your first impression of the scene using emphatic language.

Avoiding repetition (chapter 5)

Good writing means using a **variety** of **different** sentence structures and **wide** range of vocabulary that keep your reader interested in your writing! One way to do this is to avoid using the same words and structures again and again. This can be achieved by …

- using synonyms (check your dictionary or thesaurus), especially for common verbs like 'think', 'do', 'get', and 'make' or adjectives like 'good', 'bad', 'happy', 'sad'.
  Gatsby thought about Daisy a lot. = Gatsby <u>had her on his mind</u> constantly.
- using subordinate clauses, participles or gerunds
  Gatsby got home, checked the time and changed his clothes. = As soon as he got home, he checked the time before changing his clothes.
- using 'one(s)'
  He received a phone call at 10pm and a phone call at midnight. = He received a phone call at 10pm and a second one two hours later.

1. **Write down as many words as possible that can be used instead of 'good' and 'bad', 'happy' and 'sad'. Exchange your ideas with your partner and complete your own list. Then check your dictionary and/or thesaurus and add three more ideas.**

2. **The following text is a summary of a passage taken from chapter 5 of the novel. The marked words or phrases are all repetitions which could be avoided. Think of ways to improve the text by using synonyms or making any other appropriate adjustments.**

<u>Nick</u> arrives in West Egg. <u>He</u> finds all the lights in Gatsby's house blazing. <u>Gatsby</u> himself is walking toward him across the lawn. <u>Gatsby</u> invites Nick to go to Coney Island. <u>Nick</u> turns him down. <u>Gatsby</u> invites Nick for a swim in the pool. He hasn't used the <u>pool</u> all summer. Nick <u>thinks</u> it is a good idea to invite Daisy over. Gatsby <u>thinks</u> it is best to wait for a few days so that he can get Nick's grass cut. <u>He</u> offers Nick some money. <u>He</u> turns Gatsby down.
The big day arrives and it rains. Gatsby is so nervous. He <u>cannot</u> function. He <u>has not</u> slept. He is as pale as a high school boy on his first date. Life with Daisy in Louisville was so <u>happy</u> five years before; now he is terrified that even if Daisy should agree to renew their relationship it won't be the same. Daisy arrives looking very <u>good</u> in a three-cornered lavender hat. She <u>really wants to know</u> why Nick has invited her over. Nick takes Daisy inside. He <u>thinks</u> that Gatsby is <u>waiting</u> for her. But he is not <u>waiting</u> for them.

Using participle clauses (chapter 6)

One way of adding variety to your written texts is by using participle clauses. A participle clause can often replace an adverbial clause of time, reason etc.:

1. *When he saw her for the first time*, he immediately fell in love with her. (adverbial clause)
   On seeing her for the first time, he immediately fell in love with her. (participle clause)

2. You can use "having + past participle" for saying that the reason for something lies in the past:
   Having spoken to her, he had to see her again.

3. Participle constructions can also be used to describe the accompanying circumstances of an action:
   present participle: He spoke to her, *throwing* around his shirts.
   past participle: She arrived at the party, *accompanied* by her husband.

Partner A: **Underline all the participle constructions in the following sentences about chapter 6. Then rewrite the sentences using adverbial clauses.**

1. Trying to bring Gatsby's friends together for the funeral, Nick realizes that everybody has disappeared.

2. Tom and Daisy have gone away, leaving no address.

3. Shocked about their reaction, Nick desperately tries to contact any other friends.

4. Meyer Wolfshiem does not want to be involved with Gatsby, being afraid of scandals.

5. Having arrived at Gatsby's house, the three men prepare for the funeral.

6. Mr Gatz shows a picture of his son's house to the others, not realizing the darker side of Gatsby.

Partner B: **Use participle constructions to link/shorten the following sentences about chapter 6.**

1. When Nick tries to bring Gatsby's friends together for the funeral, he realizes that everybody has disappeared.

2. Tom and Daisy have gone away. They have left no address.

3. Nick is shocked about their reaction. Then he desperately tries to contact any other friends.

4. Meyer Wolfshiem does not want to be involved with Gatsby because he is afraid of scandals.

5. They arrive at Gatsby's house. Then they prepare for the funeral.

6. When Mr Gatz shows a picture of his son's house to the others, he does not realize the darker side of Gatsby.

Pairwork: **Read out your ideas to your partner and give him/her some feedback.**

Brain 28 (chapter 2 & 3)

Bei der Aufgabe Brain 28 handelt es sich um eine intensive Wortschatzarbeit, die verschiedene Lerntypen anspricht. Im Mittelpunkt stehen dabei insgesamt 28 Begriffe aus den Kapiteln 2 und 3.

Den Schülerinnen und Schüler werden die 28 Vokabeln in vier Blöcken von jeweils sieben Begriffen präsentiert. Das Ziel für jeden Schüler ist es, möglichst viele der Vokabeln zu behalten, ohne dabei mit dem Nachbarn zu kooperieren.

1. Block: Es werden die ersten sieben Begriffe vorgelesen und gleichzeitig Karten, auf denen die Vokabeln einzeln und groß genug abgedruckt sind, gezeigt.
2. Block: Ohne Kommentar werden die nächsten sieben Begriffe nur gezeigt.
3. Block: Die nächsten sieben Begriffe werden nicht gezeigt, sondern nur vorgelesen.
4. Block: Die letzten sieben Begriffe werden wieder gezeigt und vorgelesen.

Nach der Präsentation haben die Schülerinnen und Schüler fünf Minuten Zeit, individuell möglichst viele Vokabeln aus der Erinnerung heraus aufzuschreiben. Nach Ablauf der Zeit zählt jeder Schüler seine Begriffe und versucht, in Gruppen- oder Partnerarbeit seine Liste zu ergänzen. Danach erfolgt ein Abgleich im Plenum. Anschließend können einzelne Begriffe herausgegriffen werden und zu weiterer Wortschatzarbeit (Erstellung eines *semantic field*, *mind map* etc.) dienen. Denkbar ist auch das Verfassen einer *summary* der beiden Kapitel, bei der die Begriffe verwendet werden müssen.

Vokabeln für Brain 28 (aus Kapitel 2 und 3)

1. desolate 2. to perceive 3. to resent 4. solemn 5. mistress 6. anemic 7. handsome	1. dumb 2. earnest 3. to suppose 4. adorable 5. to reject 6. desperate 7. to imply
1. elaborate 2. ambiguous 3. repelled 4. to pretend 5. prosperous 6. to deny 7. to alter	1. deliberate 2. prejudice 3. approval 4. indifferent 5. reluctant 6. astonishing 7. careless

Adjectives (chapter 4)

The following adjectives are taken from chapter 4 of the novel.

1. **Look up the words you don't know. Some of the adjectives are used for describing something negative whereas some are mostly used in positive contexts. Mark them in two different colours. (Note: Some adjectives might be ambiguous.)**

gratified	frank	strained	inevitable	splendid
modest	offended	scornful	roaring	sombre
disconcerting	gorgeous	hilarious	generous	hospitable

2. **Decipher the correct opposites for the adjectives taken from chapter 4.**

generous: gr**dy

scornful: r*sp*ctf*l   or   p*l*t*

hilarious: s*r***s   or   gr*v*

inevitable: d**btf*l

modest: pr*t*nt***s   or   *mm*d*st

frank: d*sh*n*st   and   *nd*r*ct

gratified: *ns*t*sf**d

3. **Match the adjectives on the left with their correct synonyms on the right.**

roaring	marvellous
offended	troubled, disturbed
strained	entertaining
disconcerting	angry, insulted
hilarious	tense and worried
splendid	loud, exciting

4. **Choose three adjectives from the list of words in 1. and form sentences about the part of the chapter to which your words relate.**

5. **Exchange your sentences with your partner and rewrite the sentences using synonyms or opposites.**

Vocabulary/replacement (chapter 7 & 8)

1. **Read each sentence carefully. Underline the word or phrase of the sentence that can be replaced with one of your vocabulary words given in the box below (taken from chapter 7 and 8 of the novel).**

2. **Then rewrite the sentence, replacing the crossed out part of the sentence with the correct expression. You may have to add, remove, or slightly change the sentence in order for it to make sense. The first sentence has been done for you.**

3. **On a separate sheet of paper make a table that lists the new vocabulary and their German equivalents as well as English definitions.**

> relieved ■ to investigate ■ to exclaim ■ sensuous ■ to be tempted to do sth. ■ to bother
> ■ revolting ■ to persuade sb. ■ precious ■ greedy ■ malice ■ presumptuous ■ deranged

1. I'm **feeling happy** because nobody was hurt in the accident. (relieved)

   I'm relieved that nobody was hurt in the accident.

2. It was quite arrogant and disrespectful of my neighbour to assume that she was invited to our party even though she had not received an invitation.

3. The detective gave a shocking report on the crazy serial killer who stalked college students.

4. She opened her eyes and suddenly said loudly, "It isn't fair".

5. Dreaming of her full lips, he was unable to concentrate on the lecturer's words.

6. The sun was shining brightly and there was a mild breeze coming from the ocean. I was thinking about taking the day off, even though I had clients waiting for me at my office.

7. I don't want to upset her with my problems at the moment. She looks too tired.

8. A disgusting smell was in the air when she opened the door to her apartment.

9. Even though he already owned jewelry worth thousands of dollars, he stared at her diamonds.

10. I am sure he'll come to our party when you give him some good reasons for it!

11. She has never talked about her daughter before who she loved and valued very much.

12. Police are carefully examining possible links between the murders.

13. After the young man ran into her, she realized that he was not sorry but acting with meanness.

Bildnachweis

|Avenue Images GmbH, Hamburg: Les Cunliffe/agefotostock 33. |Domke, Franz-Josef, Hannover: 57. |F1online digitale Bildagentur GmbH, Frankfurt/M.: Fstop 73. |fotolia.com, New York: Maxim_Kazmin 104; Secunda-Vista 73. |Getty Images, München: Keystone-France/Gamma-Keystone 73. |Paramount Pictures: © 1974 Newdon Company © 2004 Paramount Pictures 29, 29, 29, 29, 52, 52, 52, 52, 52, 52, 52, 56. |Picture-Alliance GmbH, Frankfurt/M.: Bildagentur-online 88; PictureLux/The Hollywood Archive 3. |vario images, Bonn: 73.